THE
PORTMEIRION
BOOK OF
COUNTRY COOKING

THE
PORTMEIRION
—— BOOK OF ——
COUNTRY COOKING

EBURY PRESS · LONDON

Published by Ebury Press for Portmeirion Potteries Ltd.,
Penkhull New Road, Stoke on Trent, ST4 5DD
Ebury Press is the book division of The National Magazine Company Ltd.,
Colquhoun House, 27–37 Broadwick Street, London W1V 1FR

ISBN 0 85223 654 9

Art director: Frank Phillips
Designer: Bill Mason
Photography: Tim Imrie

Typeset in England by Chapterhouse Typesetting Ltd, Formby
Printed and bound in Italy by New Interlitho, S.p.a., Milan

CONTENTS

CHICKEN AND TARRAGON SOUP (*page 8*)

INTRODUCTION

The name Portmeirion was invented by Susan Williams-Ellis' father, Sir Clough Williams-Ellis, for his fantasy village in North Wales. When Susan and I got married, we lived in Wales and soon got involved at Portmeirion. Sir Clough wanted to build and, finding us willing, left us to manage the business side of things to make money to pay for his constructions. One way, we found, was to go in for shopkeeping in the village. Susan has studied art under Henry Moore and was particularly interested in industrial design, so we started having her designs manufactured for us to sell. This experience was very useful. It focused our attention on the importance of designing things that people actually want, and that shops can sell.

One day, when we were particularly cross with the little pottery firm we were using, but which never seemed to understand our instructions, I suggested that we should try to buy it. We did, and despite initial problems we slowly became successful, largely through Susan's flair for design. The real turning point came in 1972 with the first production of Botanic Garden. As often happens, at first there were cries of doom. No-one would buy a pattern with all those motifs. No shop would dream of stocking it. Sixteen years later we can still hardly keep up with the demand for Botanic Garden and it must be one of the best selling ceramic patterns ever.

However, even with Botanic Garden there were still ups and downs as we gradually built up a really efficient team, but for the last six years or so we have been astonishingly successful. Success has enabled us to modernise our equipment and expand into new areas such as textiles, trays and table mats.

Portmeirion is successful because all its products reflect the vitality of a single taste: that of Susan Williams-Ellis. So many things produced today are the work of committees. Sketches and projects are bandied to and fro and endlessly revised until they lose whatever life they ever had and become boringly dull. Portmeirion is not like that. Each item in the collection is as Susan intended it to be, and retains the freshness and vitality with which she infuses everything she touches. Portmeirion's creations are life enhancing and this is why people love them.

EUAN COOPER-WILLIS

Starters

Chicken and Tarragon Soup

This pale and pretty soup makes a perfect prelude to a special meal.

Serves Four

1 large chicken carcass and giblets
1 pig's trotter
2 onions, skinned and each stuck with 2 cloves
1 carrot, peeled and thinly sliced
2 garlic cloves, crushed
1 celery stick, trimmed and sliced
1 bouquet garni
350 ml (12 fl oz) dry white wine
8 peppercorns
1 bunch tarragon (use stalks in stock)
1 chicken breast fillet
150 ml (¼ pint) single cream
1 egg yolk
salt and freshly ground pepper
chopped fresh tarragon and single cream, to garnish

1 Put the chicken carcass and giblets (but not the liver) and the trotter into a large saucepan of water. Bring to the boil, skim and add the onions stuck with cloves, the carrot, garlic, celery, bouquet garni, white wine and peppercorns together with any tarragon stems.

2 Bring to the boil and simmer for 1–2 hours, skimming often and adding more water if necessary. Strain. Leave to cool, refrigerate then skim off the fat. Return to the saucepan and reduce to 750 ml (1¼ pints).

3 Cut the chicken breast into small pieces and simmer in the prepared stock for about 8 minutes, or until tender. Turn into a blender or food processor and blend until smooth.

4 Add the cream, egg yolk and a very small handful of tarragon leaves and blend just enough to make a pale green, slightly flecked mixture. Season and reheat very gently. Serve garnished with chopped tarragon and a swirl of cream.

Fresh Tomato Soup with Basil

❦

Use home grown tomatoes and basil for the best results.

❦

Serves Six

50 g (2 oz) butter or margarine
2 onions, skinned and thinly sliced
900 g (2 lb) tomatoes
45 ml (3 tbsp) plain flour
900 ml (1½ pints) chicken stock
30 ml (2 level tbsp) tomato purée
7.5 ml (1½ tsp) chopped fresh basil or 2.5 ml (½ tsp) dried
fresh basil leaves and single cream, to garnish

❦

1 Melt the butter in a saucepan, add the onions and fry gently until golden brown.
2 Meanwhile, wipe and halve the tomatoes, scoop out the seeds into a sieve placed over a bowl. Press the seeds to remove all the tomato pulp and juice; discard the seeds and reserve the juice.
3 Remove the pan from the heat. Stir in the flour and cook gently for 1 minute, stirring. Remove the pan from the heat and gradually stir in the stock. Bring to the boil slowly and continue to cook, stirring, until thickened.
4 Stir in the tomato purée, herbs and the tomatoes with reserved juice and season. Cover the pan and simmer gently for about 30 minutes.
5 Leave the soup to cool slightly, then sieve or purée in a blender or food processor. Strain into a clean pan and reheat gently. Season to taste.

Almond Soup

❦

This soup, also called white soup, dates back to medieval times when almonds were used extensively in cookery. It tastes delicate and luxurious, yet is very easy and quite economical to make.

❦

Serves Six

100 g (4 oz) ground almonds
1.4 litres (2½ pints) chicken or light veal stock
1 bay leaf
150 ml (¼ pint) single, double or whipping cream
2 egg yolks
salt and white pepper
lemon juice
25 g (1 oz) toasted flaked almonds, to serve

❦

1 Put the almonds into a saucepan and blend in the stock. Bring to the boil, stirring, then add the bay leaf and simmer for 30 minutes.
2 Remove the bay leaf, purée the soup in a blender or food processor, then return to a clean saucepan and reheat gently.
3 Blend the cream into the egg yolks in a bowl, then stir in a little of the soup. Pour back into the saucepan and heat gently, stirring, until the soup thickens. Do not allow to boil. Season with salt, pepper and lemon juice.
4 Serve the soup sprinkled with toasted almonds.

FRESH TOMATO SOUP WITH BASIL (*page 9*)

Rough Game Pâté

If you can't buy individual hare joints make two or three pâtés and freeze for a later date. Venison could be used in place of the hare.

Serves Ten–Twelve

450 g (1 lb) streaky bacon, rinded

225 g (8 oz) pig's liver

225 g (8 oz) onion

700 g (1½ lb) hare joints

225 g (8 oz) pork sausage meat

1 small orange

45 ml (3 tbsp) brandy

45 ml (3 level tbsp) chopped fresh coriander or parsley

1 egg

salt and freshly ground pepper

orange slices and fresh coriander, to garnish

1 Stretch half the bacon rashers with the back of a blunt-edged knife. Refrigerate. Coarsely mince the remaining bacon with the liver and onion then place the mixture in a large bowl.

2 Cut all the hare meat off the bone and divide into small pieces (not larger than 5 mm (¼ in) cubes). Add to the bowl with the sausage meat, grated rind of half the orange and 45 ml (3 tbsp) orange juice, the brandy, coriander, egg and plenty of seasoning. Stir well until evenly mixed. Cover tightly and refrigerate for about 8 hours or overnight.

3 Line a 1.4–1.7 litre (2½–3 pint) terrine dish with the prepared bacon rashers. Stir the pâté mixture then spoon into the lined terrine. Cover tightly with foil and stand the dish in a roasting tin with water halfway up its sides.

4 Bake at 170°C (325°F) mark 3 for 2½–3 hours, or until the juices run clear when the pâté is tested with a fine skewer. Remove from the oven; cool slightly.

5 Place a few heavy weights on top of the pâté and complete cooling. Cover and refrigerate overnight.

6 Turn out the pâté, reserving any juices to add to gravies or stocks. Slice for serving garnished with orange slices and fresh coriander.

Smoked Mackerel with Apple

This healthy starter or lunch dish is best served with warm, crusty bread. Because of its high oil content, mackerel deteriorates quickly and that is why it is widely available preserved – smoked, pickled and salted.

Serves Eight

350 g (12 oz) smoked mackerel
100 g (4 oz) celery, trimmed and finely chopped
100 g (4 oz) cucumber, skinned and finely chopped
100 g (4 oz) red eating apples, cored and chopped
150 ml (¼ pint) soured cream
30 ml (2 tbsp) lemon juice
paprika, to taste
1 small crisp lettuce, shredded

1 Skin the mackerel, then flake the flesh roughly with a fork. Discard the bones.
2 Combine the celery, cucumber, apple and mackerel in a bowl. Stir in the soured cream, lemon juice and paprika to taste.
3 Place a little lettuce in the base of 8 stemmed glasses. Divide the mackerel equally between them.
4 Garnish each glass with a lemon wedge, if liked, and sprinkle with paprika. Serve at room temperature.

Chicken Liver Mousselines with Cranberry Sauce

A delicious way to serve this substantial starter or supper dish is with small croûtes of toast or fried bread.

Serves Four

40 g (1½ oz) butter
25 g (1 oz) shallots, skinned and finely chopped
1 small garlic clove, skinned and chopped
100 g (4 oz) chicken livers
50 g (2 oz) raw chicken breast
25 g (1 oz) fresh white breadcrumbs
1 egg
75 ml (3 fl oz) double cream
salt and freshly ground pepper
parsley or chervil sprigs, to garnish

SAUCE

50 g (2 oz) cranberries
15 ml (1 tbsp) sugar
30 ml (2 tbsp) Madeira
225 ml (8 fl oz) chicken stock
40 g (1½ oz) butter, chilled

1 Melt the butter in a saucepan and use a little to grease four 100 ml (4 fl oz) ramekin dishes.
2 Fry the shallots and garlic until soft, cool slightly, then place them in a food processor with the chicken livers, chicken breast, breadcrumbs, egg, cream and seasoning. Blend to a smooth purée.
3 Spoon the purée into the ramekin dishes and cover each one with aluminium foil. Place in a small

roasting tin, and pour in enough boiling water to come three-quarters of the way up the sides of the ramekin dishes. Cook at 180°C (350°F) mark 4 for about 25 minutes or until firm to the touch. Remove from the water.

4 Meanwhile, make the sauce. Place the cranberries, sugar and Madeira in a saucepan, and boil until the liquid has reduced to 15 ml (1 tbsp). Add the stock and boil rapidly for about 5 minutes until the sauce is of a light syrupy consistency. Remove from the heat and whisk in the butter.

5 Unmould the mousses on to individual plates, spoon the sauce around and garnish with parsley.

Devilled Whitebait with Deep-fried Parsley

Coated in flour seasoned with spices, these young fish are deep fried and then eaten whole.

Serves Four

60 ml (4 tbsp) plain flour
1.25 ml (¼ tsp) curry powder
1.25 ml (¼ tsp) ground ginger
1.25 ml (¼ tsp) cayenne pepper
salt
600 g (1¼ lb) whitebait, fresh or frozen
oil, for deep-frying
15 g (½ oz) parsley sprigs
sea salt
lemon twists, to garnish

1 Sift the flour, curry powder, ginger, cayenne pepper and salt together into a large plastic bag. Put a quarter of the whitebait into the bag and shake well to coat them in the flour mixture. Lift the fish out and shake in a sieve to remove excess flour. Repeat with the remaining whitebait.

2 Heat the oil in a deep-fat fryer to 190°C (375°F). Put a single layer of whitebait into the frying basket and lower it into the pan. Fry for 2–3 minutes, shaking the basket occasionally, until the whitebait make a rustling sound as they are shaken.

3 Tip out on to a warmed plate lined with absorbent kitchen paper. Fry the remaining whitebait in the same way.

4 Allow the fat to reduce in temperature to about 186°C (365°F). Deep-fry the parsley for a few seconds until it stops sizzling. Drain on absorbent kitchen paper then sprinkle with sea salt.

5 Divide the whitebait between 4 individual warmed plates. Scatter over the parsley sprigs and garnish with the lemon twists.

DEVILLED WHITEBAIT WITH DEEP-FRIED PARSLEY (*page 13*)

INDIVIDUAL MUSSEL SOUFFLES (*page 16*)

Individual Mussel Soufflés

These soufflés make a very elegant beginning to a dinner party meant to impress. To save time, cook the mussels and mix with the sauce in advance.

Serves Four

750 g (1½ lb) fresh mussels
150 ml (¼ pint) white wine
1 garlic clove, skinned and chopped
1 shallot, skinned and chopped
1 thyme sprig
1 parsley sprig
1 bay leaf
10 ml (2 tsp) cornflour
15 ml (1 tbsp) water
2 egg yolks
25 g (1 oz) butter
15 ml (1 tbsp) lemon juice
freshly ground pepper
30 ml (2 tbsp) grated Parmesan cheese
3 egg whites

1 Scrub the mussels well and remove the beards. Tap any which have opened – if they do not close, discard them. Place the mussels in a saucepan with the wine. Cover and cook over high heat for 5–7 minutes, until all the shells have opened. Discard any closed shells.

2 Drain the mussels and return the liquid to the pan. Add the garlic, shallot and herbs, and boil rapidly until reduced to 150 ml (¼ pint). Strain through a muslin cloth and reserve.

3 Remove the mussels from their shells. Combine the cornflour, water and egg yolks, and add it to the reduced liquid in a small saucepan. Cook gently, stirring, until thickened. Stir in half the butter, then add the lemon juice and pepper to taste.

4 Grease four 175 ml (6 fl oz) ramekin dishes and coat the sides with Parmesan cheese. Chill.

5 Whisk the egg whites until stiff, then fold them into the sauce mixture until evenly combined. Spoon half the mixture into the prepared ramekin dishes. Sprinkle the mussels on top and finish with the remaining soufflé mixture.

6 Place the ramekins on a preheated baking tray and bake at 180°C (350°F) mark 4 for about 20 minutes until risen and golden. Serve immediately.

Meat
Main Course Dishes

Beef with Spring Vegetables

A classic way of cooking beef that had been preserved for the winter months by salting. Order the meat in advance and check whether it needs soaking.

Serves Six

1.6 kg (3½ lb) lean salted brisket or silverside of beef

bouquet garni of 1 bay leaf, 6 parsley stalks, small sprig of rosemary, sprig of thyme

6 black peppercorns, lightly crushed

2 small onions, quartered and a clove stuck in each quarter

1 carrot, peeled and quartered

2 small turnips, quartered

2 celery sticks, trimmed and chopped

1 leek, trimmed and chopped

12 small carrots

peas and mashed potatoes or dumplings, to serve

1 Place the beef in a large saucepan, add just enough water to cover and bring slowly to the boil. Remove the scum from the surface, add the bouquet garni, peppercorns, onion, carrot quarters, turnip, celery and leek. Lower the heat and simmer very gently for about 2 hours. Add the small carrots and simmer gently for a further 30–40 minutes or until the carrots are tender.

2 Carefully transfer the beef and small carrots to a warmed serving plate and keep warm. Strain the cooking liquor and remove the fat from the surface. Boil the liquid to reduce slightly then pour into a warmed sauceboat.

3 Serve the beef surrounded by the carrots, accompanied by peas and mashed potatoes or dumplings, with the sauce handed separately.

Brown Ragout of Lamb

❦

If broad beans are not available, peas or flageolet
beans could be used instead.

❦

Serves Six

75 g (3 oz) butter, diced

900 g (2 lb) leg of lamb, cut into 2.5 cm (1 in) pieces

750 ml (1¼ pints) brown stock, preferably veal

1 onion, unskinned, stuck with 4 cloves

salt and freshly ground pepper

3 parsley sprigs

2 thyme sprigs

2 bay leaves

1 rosemary sprig

3 carrots, cut into even sized pieces

12 small onions, skinned

100 g (4 oz) button mushrooms

squeeze of lemon juice

75 g (3 oz) shelled broad beans, cooked, to serve

flesh of 2 large firm tomatoes, cut into strips and 30 ml
(2 tbsp) finely chopped fresh parsley, to garnish

1 Melt 40 g (1½ oz) of the butter in a large heavy frying pan, add the lamb in batches and cook until an even golden brown. Transfer to a casserole using a slotted spoon. Reserve the butter in the pan.

2 Put the stock in a saucepan with the unpeeled onion, seasoning and herbs and bring to the boil. Pour over the lamb, cover tightly and cook at 180°C (350°F) mark 4 for about 1 hour, stirring occasionally.

3 Meanwhile, add another 15 g (½ oz) butter to the frying pan and melt. Add the carrots and small onions and fry until lightly browned.

4 Drain on absorbent kitchen paper then stir into the casserole. Cover tightly again and cook for a further 30 minutes. Cook the mushrooms in the remaining butter with a squeeze of lemon juice. Drain on absorbent kitchen paper.

5 Remove the onion stuck with cloves from the casserole, then stir in the mushrooms and cook, uncovered, for 10 minutes. Using a slotted spoon, lift the meat and vegetables from the dish and keep warm. Boil the liquid until it is reduced to about 400 ml (14 fl oz), then pour into a warmed jug.

6 Arrange the meat on a large warmed serving plate with the vegetables, adding the broad beans, and pour over some sauce. Garnish with the tomato flesh and the parsley. Serve, with the rest of the sauce handed separately.

BROWN RAGOUT OF LAMB (*opposite*)

Roast Sirloin with Fresh Horseradish Sauce

---❧---

This classic English dish is reputed to have been knighted by an English king after he had dined particularly well off a roasted loin of beef. For a meal 'fit for a king' serve with Yorkshire puddings and roast potatoes.

---❧---

Serves Six

1.1 kg (2½ lb) boned and rolled sirloin of beef
175 ml (6 fl oz) red wine
450 ml (¾ pint) brown stock, preferably veal
salt and freshly ground pepper

SAUCE

150 ml (¼ pint) whipping cream
45 ml (3 tbsp) freshly grated horseradish
about 22.5 ml (1½ tbsp) lemon juice
1.25–2.5 ml (¼–½ tsp) prepared English mustard
salt and white pepper
pinch of sugar (optional)

---❧---

1 Place the meat, fat side up, on a rack placed in a roasting tin. Cook at 230°C (450°F) mark 8 for 15 minutes, then reduce the temperature to 170°C (325°F) mark 3 and cook for about a further 40 minutes for rare beef, basting once or twice.
2 Meanwhile, blend all the ingredients for the sauce and spoon into a serving bowl.
3 Leave the beef, still on the rack, in a warm place to settle. Drain off the excess fat from the roasting tin. Place the tin over a medium heat and stir in the red wine, dislodging the sediment stuck in the bottom of the tin.
4 Boil until almost completely evaporated, then stir in the stock and boil until reduced to 200 ml (7 fl oz). Season and pour into a sauceboat. Serve the beef accompanied by the gravy and horseradish sauce.

Roast Pork with Blue Cheese Sauce

---❧---

In this dish the roast pork flavour is complemented by the surprisingly easy-to-make cheese sauce. Stilton cheese is used in this recipe, although Roquefort or Danish blue can be substituted.

---❧---

Serves Four–Six

1 kg (2 lb) loin of pork
12 sage leaves
vegetable oil
salt and freshly ground pepper
60 ml (4 tbsp) hot water or vegetable water
150 ml (¼ pint) sour cream
75 g (3 oz) Stilton cheese, crumbled

---❧---

1 Wipe the meat with damp absorbent kitchen paper. Slightly loosen the skin and fat from the meat at both ends of the joint and tuck the sage leaves underneath. Brush the skin with oil and sprinkle with salt.
2 Roast at 180°C (350°F) mark 4 for 35 minutes

per 500 g (1 lb) plus 35 minutes. Transfer to a warmed serving dish and keep hot while preparing the sauce.

3 Pour off all but 30 ml (2 tbsp) of the fat from the roasting tin. Pour the remaining 30 ml (2 tbsp) and the sediment into a small pan with the water. Bring to the boil, stirring. Reduce the heat and stir in the sour cream and Stilton cheese. Stir over gentle heat until the cheese has melted. Do not allow to boil. Adjust the seasoning.

4 Carve the meat into thin slices and serve the sauce separately.

Spiced Beef

Spiced beef is traditional Christmas fare in Leicester-shire and parts of Yorkshire. Once cooked it can be kept, well wrapped, in the refrigerator for 1–2 weeks.

Serves Eight–Ten

1.8 kg (4 lb) lean, boned topside or silverside of beef
100 g (4 oz) coarse sea salt
15 ml (1 tbsp) crushed juniper berries
15 ml (1 tbsp) crushed black peppercorns
15 ml (1 tbsp) whole allspice
1 blade of mace
1 bay leaf
5 ml (1 tsp) chopped fresh thyme
75 g (3 oz) dark brown sugar
7.5 ml (1½ tsp) saltpetre
150 ml (¼ pint) red wine

TO SERVE
horseradish sauce
beetroot
thinly sliced brown bread and butter or crusty bread
pickled onions and other pickles

———— ⚘ ————

1 Rub all the surfaces of the beef with the salt, roll the meat up and place it in a casserole. Cover and leave in a cool place overnight.

2 Crush the spices and herbs together, then crush with the sugar and saltpetre. Dry the surface of the meat with absorbent kitchen paper. Tip any liquid from the casserole. Rub the spice mixture all over the meat, roll it up and return it to the casserole. Cover and leave in a cool place for 9 days, turning the meat daily and rubbing in the spice mixture.

3 Dry the beef well with absorbent kitchen paper, then return it to the casserole. Pour over the wine. Cover tightly and cook at 170°C (325°F) mark 3 for about 3 hours or until the beef is tender.

4 Remove from the oven and leave in a cool place for about 3 hours. Drain the meat, place it between two boards, and put heavy weights on top. Leave in a cool place for 24 hours.

5 Carve into thin slices and serve with horseradish sauce, beetroot and thin brown bread and butter or crusty bread, pickled onions and other pickles.

ROAST SIRLOIN WITH FRESH HORSERADISH SAUCE (*page 20*)

PARSON'S VENISON (*page 24*)

Parson's Venison

❧

Marinating a leg of lamb in lightly spiced red wine transforms the flesh into a more full-flavoured meat reminiscent of venison.

❧

Serves Four–Six

25 g (1 oz) dripping or butter
1 small onion, skinned and finely chopped
100 g (4 oz) mushrooms, chopped
100 g (4 oz) ham, chopped
30 ml (2 tbsp) snipped chives
salt and freshly ground pepper
1.8–2 kg (4–4½ lb) leg of lamb, skinned and boned

MARINADE

200 ml (7 fl oz) red wine
75 ml (3 fl oz) tawny port
6 juniper berries, crushed
1.25 ml (¼ tsp) ground allspice
30 ml (2 tbsp) vegetable oil
45 ml (3 tbsp) red wine vinegar
1 bay leaf
1.25 ml (¼ tsp) freshly grated nutmeg
watercress sprigs, to garnish

1 Melt half the dripping or butter in a saucepan, add the onion and mushrooms and cook, stirring frequently, until the onions are soft but not browned. Stir in the ham, chives and seasoning and leave to cool.

2 Season the lamb inside and out with black pepper, then spread the onion mixture over the inside. Roll up tightly and tie securely. Place in a casserole.

3 Mix the marinade ingredients together, pour over the lamb, cover and leave in a cool place for 24 hours, turning the joint over occasionally. Remove the meat from the marinade, drain and dry.

4 Melt the remaining dripping or butter in a large frying pan. Add the meat and brown on all sides over medium to high heat. Transfer to a casserole.

5 Pour the marinade into the frying pan, bring to the boil, then pour over the meat. Cover, then cook at 180°C (350°F) mark 4 for 1¾–2 hours until the meat is tender, basting occasionally with the marinade.

6 Transfer the meat to a warmed plate. Skim the fat from the surface of the liquid, then boil the liquid rapidly until reduced and slightly thickened. Season to taste with salt and pepper. Garnish the meat with watercress and serve with the gravy.

Oxtail Stew

❧

This stew can be served as it is, straight from the pot with carrots, small onions and leeks.

❧

Serves Four

25 g (1 oz) beef dripping, or vegetable oil

50 g (2 oz) bacon, chopped

1 large or 2 small oxtails, chopped

1 large onion, skinned and finely chopped

2 carrots, peeled and chopped

1 celery stick, trimmed and chopped

1 large leek, trimmed and chopped

bouquet garni of 1 bay leaf, a sprig of thyme, 4 parsley sprigs and a sprig of lovage

salt and freshly ground pepper

300 ml (½ pint) brown ale

300 ml (½ pint) brown stock, preferably veal

finely chopped fresh parsley, to garnish

DUMPLINGS

100 g (4 oz) self-raising flour

salt and pepper

50 g (2 oz) shredded suet or cold diced butter

2.5 ml (½ tsp) creamed horseradish (optional)

30 ml (2 tbsp) water

225 ml (8 fl oz) brown stock, preferably veal, or water

1 Heat the dripping or oil in a large heavy-based saucepan, add the bacon and oxtail pieces, a few at a time, and cook until beginning to brown. Remove with a slotted spoon and reserve.

2 Add the vegetables to the pan and cook over a low heat for about 3 minutes, stirring frequently, until the onion is beginning to soften but not brown.

3 Return the oxtail and bacon to the vegetables. Add the bouquet garni, seasoning, ale and stock and bring to the boil. Reduce the heat so the liquid barely moves, cover tightly and cook slowly for 2½–3 hours until the oxtail is very tender. Skim all fat off the surface.

4 About 25 minutes before the end of the cooking, combine all the ingredients for the dumplings except the stock and mix to a soft, but not sticky, dough with the water.

5 Divide into 8 pieces and roll into small balls using floured hands. Bring the stock or water to the boil in a large saucepan; season if using water. Add the dumplings and poach for 15–20 minutes until cooked. Remove from the pan with a slotted spoon, draining well. Place the dumplings on top of the stew and sprinkle with parsley. Serve at once.

Braised Beef with Chestnuts and Celery

This well-flavoured casserole, which dates from the eighteenth century, would have been made in the late autumn and winter when both celery and fresh chestnuts were available. It could be made at any time of the year nowadays using imported celery and where necessary canned or reconstituted dried chestnuts.

Serves Six

18 chestnuts, fresh, drained canned or reconstituted dried

30 ml (2 tbsp) beef dripping

2 bacon slices, rinded and chopped

900 g (2 lb) stewing steak, cut into cubes

1 onion, skinned and chopped

15 ml (1 tbsp) plain flour

300 ml (½ pint) brown ale

300 ml (½ pint) brown stock, preferably veal

pinch of freshly grated nutmeg

juice and finely grated rind of 1 orange

salt and freshly ground pepper

3 celery sticks, trimmed and sliced

finely chopped fresh parsley, to garnish

1 If using fresh chestnuts, slit the skins, then cook the chestnuts in simmering water for about 7 minutes. Peel off the thick outer skin and thin inner skin while still warm, removing from the water one at a time.

2 Melt the dripping in a large frying pan, add the bacon and beef in batches and cook, stirring occasionally, until browned. Remove the meat with a slotted spoon and transfer to a casserole dish.

3 Add the onion to the pan and fry, stirring, until softened. Drain off most of the fat and reserve. Sprinkle in the flour and cook, stirring, for 1–2 minutes.

4 Stir in the brown ale, stock, nutmeg, orange juice and half the rind and the seasoning. Bring to the boil, stir well to dislodge the sediment. Add to the casserole with the fresh or dried chestnuts. Cover with the lid and cook at 170°C (325°F) mark 3 for about 45 minutes.

5 Meanwhile, heat the reserved fat in a saucepan, add the celery and fry lightly. Add to the casserole after the 45 minutes cooking time, re-cover and cook for about 1 hour. (If using canned chestnuts, add them after 30 minutes, re-cover the casserole and continue cooking for the remaining 30 minutes.)

6 Serve with the remaining orange rind and the parsley sprinkled over the top.

BRAISED BEEF WITH CHESTNUTS AND CELERY (*opposite*)

Veal and Kidney Pie

For a change, top this pie filling with bought flaky pastry – you'll need a 375 g (13 oz) packet.

900 g (2 lb) stewing veal, trimmed and cut into 2.5 cm (1 in) cubes

juice of 1 lemon

6.25 ml (1¼ level tsp) dried tarragon

salt and freshly ground pepper

225 g (8 oz) lambs' kidneys

350 g (12 oz) leeks

40 g (1½ oz) butter or margarine

40 g (1½ oz) plain white flour

30 ml (2 tbsp) single cream

fresh tarragon, to garnish (optional)

PASTRY

125 g (4 oz) plain wholemeal flour mixed with 225 g (8 oz) plain white flour

1 egg, beaten

225 g (8 oz) butter or margarine

1 Place the veal in a saucepan with 900 ml (1½ pints) water, 15 ml (1 tbsp) lemon juice, 5 ml (1 level tsp) tarragon and seasoning. Cover and simmer until just tender (about 1–1¼ hours).

2 Meanwhile, cut the kidneys into bite-sized pieces, discarding skin and core. Trim the leeks, slice into 1 cm (½ in) thick rounds, rinse and drain.

3 Stir the kidneys and leeks into the saucepan. Cover and simmer for a further 8–10 minutes. Strain off the liquor and reserve. Spoon the veal mixture into a 26.5 cm (10½ in) pie plate. To make

the sauce, mix the fat and flour with 600 ml (1 pint) reserved stock. Off the heat, stir in 15 ml (1 tbsp) lemon juice, 1.25 ml (¼ level tsp) tarragon, the cream and seasoning. Pour over the veal; cool.

5 Prepare the pastry. Using a fork cut 225 g (8 oz) margarine into the wholemeal flour and plain flour mixture; or rub 225 g (8 oz) butter into the flours. Bind to a dough with 75 ml (5 tbsp) water. Wrap and chill for 30 minutes.

6 Roll out the pastry and use to top the pie. Glaze with the beaten egg.

7 Bake at 190°C (375°F) mark 5 for about 40 minutes, or until well browned. Garnish with fresh tarragon, if available.

Fish
Main Course Dishes

Poacher's Fish Cakes

Fish cakes have been a popular, quick dish since Victorian times. The type of cooked fish used can be varied according to what is available. More elaborate recipes also include a thick white sauce, which makes the cakes more like croquettes.

Serves Four

225 g (8 oz) potatoes, cooked
50 g (2 oz) butter
350 g (12 oz) salmon, cooked and flaked
15 ml (1 tbsp) finely chopped fresh thyme
squeeze of lemon juice
salt and freshly ground pepper
cayenne pepper
1–2 eggs, beaten
45 ml (3 tbsp) seasoned plain flour
50 g (2 oz) dried breadcrumbs
vegetable oil, for frying
watercress sprigs and lemon slices, to garnish

1 Purée the potatoes or mash them well. Put into a saucepan, preferably non-stick, and heat gently, stirring, to dry them out completely. Beat in the butter with a wooden spoon.

2 Remove the pan from the heat and beat in the salmon, thyme, lemon juice and seasonings, and just enough egg to bind together. Leave to cool, then cover and chill.

3 Divide into 4 or 8 portions, then, with floured hands, shape each portion into a flat cake. Coat in seasoned flour then the remaining egg, then the breadcrumbs.

4 Heat the oil in a frying pan, add the fish cakes and fry, turning once, until crisp and golden. Drain on absorbent paper. Serve garnished with watercress and lemon slices.

VEAL AND KIDNEY PIE (*page 28*)

SPECIAL PARSLEY FISH PIE (*page 32*)

Special Parsley Fish Pie

Enriched with cream, this special version of the popular family dish also contains the added attraction of prawns. Pipe the potatoes for the perfect finishing touch.

Serves Four

450 g (1 lb) whiting fillet

300 ml (½ pint) milk, plus 90 ml (6 tbsp)

1 bay leaf

6 peppercorns

1 onion, skinned and sliced

salt

65 g (2½ oz) butter

45 ml (3 tbsp) plain flour

freshly ground pepper

2 eggs, hard-boiled and chopped

150 ml (¼ pint) single cream

30 ml (2 tbsp) chopped fresh parsley

100 g (4 oz) peeled prawns

900 g (2 lb) potatoes, peeled

1 egg, beaten, to glaze

1 Place the whiting in a saucepan and pour over the 300 ml (½ pint) milk. Add the bay leaf, peppercorns, onion and a pinch of salt. Bring to the boil and simmer for 10 minutes until just tender.

2 Lift from the pan, flake the flesh and remove the skin and bones. Strain the cooking liquid and reserve.

3 Make the sauce. Melt 40 g (1½ oz) of the butter in the saucepan, add the flour and cook gently, stir-

ring, for 1–2 minutes. Remove from the heat and gradually blend in the reserved cooking liquid. Bring to the boil, stirring constantly, then simmer for 3 minutes until thickened. Add salt and pepper to taste.

4 Add the eggs to the sauce with the cream, fish, parsley and prawns. Check the seasoning, then spoon the mixture into a 29.5 cm (11 in) oval baking dish.

5 Meanwhile, boil the potatoes, drain and mash without any liquid. Heat the 90 ml (6 tbsp) of milk and remaining butter and beat into the potatoes with salt and pepper to taste.

6 Spoon the potatoes into a piping bag and pipe across the fish mixture. Alternatively, spoon the potato over the fish and roughen the surface with a fork.

7 Bake in the oven at 200°C (400°F) mark 6, for 10–15 minutes, until the potato is set. Brush the beaten egg over the pie. Return to the oven for a further 15 minutes until golden brown.

Cockle and Leek Pies

❧

Serve these tasty pies straight from the oven.

❧

Serves Four

grated rind and juice of 1 lemon
350 g (12 oz) shelled cooked cockles – about 600 ml
(1 pint) – well rinsed
25 g (1 oz) butter
350 g (12 oz) leeks, trimmed and thickly sliced
30 ml (2 tbsp) plain flour
150 ml (¼ pint) milk
198 g (7 oz) sweetcorn kernels, drained
pinch of freshly grated nutmeg
freshly ground pepper
212 g (7½ oz) packet puff pastry, thawed

❧

1 Stir the grated rind and 30 ml (2 tbsp) lemon juice into the cockles.

2 Heat the butter in a medium saucepan, add the leeks and fry gently for 1–2 minutes. Sprinkle over the flour. Cook, stirring, for 1–2 minutes before adding the milk, sweetcorn and nutmeg. Add pepper to taste. Allow to cool.

3 Stir in the cockles and juices. Divide the mixture between four scallop shells.

4 Roll out the pastry, divide into four and use to cover the fillings. Pressing down at the edges, trim the pastry, leaving an extra 5 mm (¼ inch) all round. Pull the back of a knife through the pastry at regular intervals to create a scalloped edge.

5 Bake in the oven at 200°C (400°F) mark 6 for about 30 minutes or until well risen and golden.

Herrings with Mustard Sauce

❧

The piquancy of the sauce in this Cornish dish is a perfect foil to the richness of the herrings.

❧

Serves Four

4 herrings, cleaned, heads removed
salt and freshly ground pepper
lemon juice, to taste

SAUCE

10 ml (2 tsp) mustard powder
2 egg yolks
50 g (2 oz) butter, diced
30 ml (2 tbsp) soured cream
salt and white pepper
a selection of large capers, silverskin onions and
gherkins cut into fan shapes, to serve

❧

1 Season the herrings inside and out with salt, pepper and lemon juice. Grill for 3–5 minutes on each side.

2 Meanwhile, prepare the sauce. Blend the mustard with the egg yolks in a bowl, then place over a saucepan of hot water and whisk until creamy. Gradually whisk in the butter until it has all been incorporated and the sauce is thick. Remove from the heat and whisk in the cream. Season.

3 Place the herrings on warmed serving plates, spoon the sauce to one side of the fish. Serve with a selection of large capers, silverskin onions and gherkins cut into fan shapes.

BAKED TROUT WITH HAZELNUTS AND DILL (*page 36*)

GRILLED MACKEREL WITH SAGE SAUCE (*page 36*)

Grilled Mackerel with Sage Sauce

This is a delicious way to serve mackerel; it is also very quick and easy to prepare.

Serves Four

4 mackerel, cleaned
salt and freshly ground pepper
150 ml (¼ pint) olive oil
30 ml (2 tbsp) lemon juice
75 ml (3 fl oz) dry white wine
75 ml (3 fl oz) dry vermouth
5 ml (1 tsp) very finely chopped fresh sage

1 Cut the fins from the mackerel and cut 3 diagonal slits in the skin across both sides of the fish. Season the fish inside and out, then place in a dish large enough to hold them in a single layer.
2 Mix the oil, lemon juice and wine together and pour over the fish. Cover and leave to marinate in a cool place for 1½ hours, turning the fish occasionally.
3 Remove the mackerel from the marinade. Cook under a hot grill for 5–8 minutes each side, depending on the thickness of the fish, until the flesh flakes easily. Transfer to a warm dish, cover and keep hot.
4 Carefully remove the oil from the top of the marinade. Pour the cooking juices into a saucepan, add the vermouth and sage leaves and simmer for 2–3 minutes. Season to taste and pour over the mackerel.

Baked Trout with Hazelnuts and Dill

This is a delicious way to cook trout. The fish are baked in wine and seasoned with dill, then served with hazelnuts and butter.

Serves Four

4 trout, about 275 g (10 oz) each, cleaned
40 ml (8 tsp) lemon juice
salt and freshly ground pepper
dill sprigs
100 ml (4 fl oz) dry white wine
1 shallot, skinned and finely chopped
75 g (3 oz) hazelnuts
50 g (2 oz) butter
lemon slices and dill, to garnish

1 Cut the fins from the fish then sprinkle 30 ml (6 tsp) of the lemon juice over the skin and the cavities. Season inside and out and put a sprig of dill in each cavity. Place the trout in a lasagne or baking dish large enough to hold them tightly in one layer. Pour over the wine and add the shallot. Cover the dish with greased greaseproof paper, then bake at 180°C (350°F) mark 4 for 20–25 minutes or until the flesh flakes easily.
2 Meanwhile, place the hazelnuts under a moderately hot grill for about 5 minutes or until the skins dry out and flake. Rub off the skins and chop. Melt the butter, add the hazelnuts and cook over moderately high heat, stirring frequently, until

golden brown. Add the remaining lemon juice and seasoning.

3 Carefully transfer the trout to 4 warmed serving plates. Boil the cooking juices rapidly until reduced to about 45 ml (3 tbsp). Spoon the juices, hazelnuts and butter over the fish. Serve at once.

Stuffed Plaice with Lemon Sauce

⩊

The plaice in this recipe is filled with a mouthwatering mushroom stuffing with green peppercorns – unripe black peppercorns pickled in brine. Serve with saffron rice and green beans.

⩊

Serves Four

4 small whole plaice, cleaned
65 g (2½ oz) butter
100 g (4 oz) button mushrooms, finely chopped
100 g (4 oz) white breadcrumbs
90 ml (6 tbsp) chopped fresh parsley
45 ml (3 tbsp) crushed green peppercorns
finely grated rind and juice of 2 lemons
1.25 ml (¼ tsp) mustard powder
salt and freshly ground pepper
1 egg, beaten
150 ml (¼ pint) dry white wine
25 g (1 oz) plain flour
60 ml (4 tbsp) single cream
lemon slices and parsley sprigs, to garnish

1 With the white skin uppermost, cut down the backbone of each of the four plaice. Carefully make a pocket on each side of the backbone by easing the white flesh from the bone.

2 Make the stuffing. Beat 15 g (½ oz) of the butter until softened, then add the mushrooms, breadcrumbs, parsley, 30 ml (2 tbsp) of the peppercorns, lemon rind, mustard and salt and pepper to taste. Mix well and moisten with the egg and a little of the lemon juice.

3 Spoon the stuffing carefully into the pockets in the fish. Then place the fish in a single layer in the buttered baking dish. Pour the wine around the fish and cover loosely with foil. Cook in the oven at 190°C (375°F) mark 5 for 30 minutes.

4 Remove the fish from the dish and place on a warmed serving dish, reserving cooking juices. Cover and keep warm in the oven turned to its lowest setting.

5 Make the sauce. Melt the remaining butter in a saucepan, add the flour and cook gently, stirring, for 1–2 minutes. Remove from the heat and gradually blend in the fish cooking juices, 150 ml (¼ pint) of water and the remaining lemon juice. Bring to the boil, stirring constantly, then lower the heat and stir in the remaining peppercorns and cream.

6 To serve the sauce, taste and adjust the seasoning, then pour into a warmed sauceboat. Garnish the fish and serve.

Summer Poached Salmon

*Cold poached salmon makes an impressive centrepiece
for a special occasion. Pay particular attention to the
garnishing and allow yourself a little extra time for
those important finishing touches. The result can look
spectacular.*

Makes Fifteen Portions

**1 small salmon, about 1.8 kg (4 lb), with tail and fins
trimmed and eyes removed
150 ml (¼ pint) dry white wine
1 onion, skinned and sliced
1 bay leaf
salt and freshly ground pepper
300 ml (½ pint) liquid aspic jelly
cucumber slices, lemon twists, whole prawns and
endive, to garnish
mayonnaise, to serve**

1 Place the salmon in a fish kettle. Pour over the
wine and enough water just to cover the fish. Add
the onion, bay leaf, salt and pepper. Bring slowly to
the boil, cover and simmer for 25 minutes.

2 Lift the salmon out of the cooking liquid; cool
for 2–3 hours. Ease off the skin and place the fish
on a serving platter.

3 As the aspic begins to set, brush some over the
fish. Leave to set in a cool place for 1–1½ hours.
Coat with several layers of aspic.

4 Garnish with prawns and cucumber slices.
Brush more aspic on top. Arrange endive, chicory,
sliced cucumber and lemon on the side of the dish
and serve with mayonnaise.

SUMMER POACHED SALMON (*opposite*)

Salmon Kedgeree

Kedgeree, sometimes also called khichri, is a rice dish of Anglo-Indian origin. In the days of the Raj it was very popular for breakfast, made with smoked fish rather than the fresh salmon used here. Original recipes for kedgeree are made with curry powder or curry spices and the rice can be quite hot and spicy, however, the delicate flavour of fresh salmon would be overpowered by pungent spices, so they are not used here.

Serves Six
350 g (12 oz) salmon
150 ml (¼ pint) dry white wine
2 small onions, skinned and chopped
1 carrot, peeled and sliced
1 celery stick, trimmed and chopped
15 ml (1 tbsp) lemon juice
6 peppercorns
1 bouquet garni
salt and freshly ground pepper
350 g (12 oz) long-grain rice
50 g (2 oz) butter
7.5 ml (1½ tsp) English mustard powder
3 eggs, hard-boiled and quartered
cayenne pepper, to finish
celery leaves or parsley sprigs, to garnish

1 Put the salmon in a saucepan, pour in the wine and enough water to cover the fish. Add half of the chopped onions, the carrot, celery, lemon juice, peppercorns, bouquet garni and 5 ml (1 tsp) salt.

2 Bring slowly to the boil, then remove from the heat. Cover tightly and cool.

3 Cook the rice in a saucepan of boiling salted water for 15–20 minutes until tender.

4 Meanwhile, remove the salmon from the liquid and flake the flesh, discarding skin and any bones. Strain the cooking liquid and reserve.

5 Melt half the butter in a large frying pan, add the remaining onion and fry gently until soft. Drain the rice thoroughly, then add to the onion with the remaining butter. Toss gently to coat in the butter and stir in the mustard powder.

6 Add the flaked salmon and the hard-boiled eggs and a few spoonfuls of the strained cooking liquid to moisten. Heat through. Shake the pan and toss the ingredients gently so that the salmon and eggs do not break up.

7 Transfer to a warmed serving dish and sprinkle with cayenne to taste. Serve immediately, garnished with celery leaves.

Creamy Fish Casserole

This layered casserole needs no other accompaniment than a seasonal green vegetable. If liked, serve ice-cold dry cider with the meal.

Serves Four–Six

700 g (1½ lb) hake, skinned and cut into bite-sized pieces
30 ml (2 tbsp) plain flour
salt and freshly ground pepper
40 g (1½ oz) butter
15 ml (1 tbsp) vegetable oil
600 ml (1 pint) dry cider
2 bay leaves, crumbled
900 g (2 lb) old floury potatoes, scrubbed
150 ml (¼ pint) single cream
30 ml (2 tbsp) chopped fresh parsley

1 Coat the pieces of hake in the flour seasoned with salt and pepper to taste.
2 Melt 25 g (1 oz) of the butter with the oil in a frying pan, add the pieces of hake and fry gently until golden on all sides. Remove from the pan with a slotted spoon and set aside.
3 Pour the cider into the frying pan and stir to dislodge the sediment from the bottom and sides of the pan. Add the bay leaves and salt and pepper. Bring to the boil and simmer for a few minutes, then pour into a jug.
4 Blanch the potatoes in their skins in boiling salted water for 10 minutes. Drain, leave until cool enough to handle, then peel off the skins and slice.

5 Put half the fish in the bottom of a small casserole or baking dish. Stir the cream into the cider mixture, then pour half over the fish.
6 Cover with half the potato slices, overlapping them so that they cover the fish completely. Sprinkle with half the parsley. Put the remaining fish on top of the potatoes, then pour over the remaining cider and cream.
7 Cover with the remaining potato slices as before, then dot with the remaining butter. Cook in the oven at 190°C (375°F) mark 5 for 45 minutes. Sprinkle the remaining parsley over the top before serving.

Poultry and Game
Main Course Dishes

Parsley Chicken with Cashew

A mildly aromatic dish with crunchy cashew nuts and lemon tang.

Serves Eight

50 g (2 oz) creamed coconut
bunch of fresh parsley
225 g (8 oz) onion, skinned and sliced
8 chicken breast fillets, about 100 g (4 oz) each
60 ml (4 tbsp) plain flour
30 ml (2 tbsp) *each* ground coriander and cumin
10 ml (2 tsp) ground turmeric
salt and freshly ground pepper
60 ml (4 tbsp) vegetable oil plus a little extra
25 g (1 oz) butter
150 g (5 oz) salted cashew nuts
600 ml (1 pint) chicken stock
60 ml (4 tbsp) lemon juice

1 Break up the coconut and dissolve in 150 ml (¼ pint) boiling water. Chop the parsley to give about 90 ml (6 tbsp). Split each chicken breast to give two thinner fillets. Mix together the flour, spices and seasoning. Use to coat the chicken.

2 Heat 60 ml (4 tbsp) oil and the butter in a large sauté pan. Brown the chicken pieces half at a time; remove from pan.

3 Add the onion and 125 g (4 oz) nuts with a little more oil if necessary and lightly brown, stirring frequently. Mix in any remaining flour followed by the coconut, water, the stock, 75 ml (5 level tbsp) parsley and the lemon juice. Return the chicken to the pan. Bring to the boil, cover and simmer for about 20 minutes, or until the chicken is quite tender, stirring occasionally.

4 Uncover and bubble down the juices until slightly thickened. Adjust seasoning and sprinkle with the remaining chopped parsley and nuts.

Cornish Caudle Chicken Pie

❧

Caudle refers to the cream and egg mixture that is poured into the pie near the end of the cooking. The quantity of pastry will give just a thin covering, a larger amount can be used if preferred.

❧

Serves Four

50 g (2 oz) butter

1 onion, skinned and finely chopped

4 chicken legs, about 100 g (4 oz) each, boned

20 g (¾ oz) fresh parsley leaves, finely chopped

4 spring onions, trimmed and chopped

salt and freshly ground pepper

150 ml (¼ pint) milk

150 ml (¼ pint) soured cream

212 g (7½ oz) packet puff pastry, thawed

beaten egg, for glazing

150 ml (¼ pint) double cream

1 egg, beaten

❧

1 Melt half the butter in a frying pan, add the onion and cook over a low heat, stirring occasionally, until softened but not browned. Transfer to a 26.5 cm (10½ in) pie plate using a slotted spoon.

2 Add the remaining butter to the pan, add the chicken and cook until evenly browned. Arrange on top of the onion in a single layer. Stir the parsley, spring onions, seasoning, milk and soured cream into the pan and bring to the boil. Simmer for 2–3 minutes, then pour over the chicken.

3 Cover with foil and cook at 180°C (350°F) mark

4 for about 30 minutes. Remove from the oven and leave to cool.

4 Meanwhile, roll out the pastry on a lightly floured surface until about 2.5 cm (1 inch) larger all round than the pie dish. Leave the pastry to relax while the filling is cooling.

5 Cut off a strip from all round the edge of the pastry. Place the strip on the rim of the pie dish, moisten, then place the pastry lid on top. Crimp the edges, make a small hole in the top and insert a small funnel of aluminium foil.

6 Brush the top of the pie with beaten egg and bake for 15–20 minutes at 220°C (425°F) mark 7 until a light golden brown. Reduce the temperature to 180°C (350°F) mark 4.

7 Beat the cream into the egg, then strain into a jug and pour into the pie through the foil funnel. Remove the funnel, shake the dish to distribute the cream and return the pie to the oven for about 5 minutes. Remove from the oven and leave to stand in a warm place for 5–10 minutes before serving warm, or leave to cool completely and serve cold.

Chicken with Cumin and Cider

❦

A fragrant, fruity dish with a hint of spice.

❦

Serves Four

15 ml (1 tbsp) vegetable oil
50 g (2 oz) butter or margarine
4 chicken leg portions
2 small cooking apples, peeled and sliced
1 small onion, skinned and sliced
5 ml (1 tsp) ground cumin
15 ml (1 tbsp) plain flour
300 ml (½ pint) chicken stock
150 ml (¼ pint) dry cider
salt and freshly ground pepper
1 large red-skinned eating apple

❦

1 Heat the oil and 25 g (1 oz) butter in a large saucepan or frying pan, add the chicken joints and fry until golden. Remove from the pan.

2 Add the cooking apples and onion to the pan, cook for 3 minutes, then stir in the cumin and flour and cook for 1 minute, stirring. Remove from the heat and gradually stir in the stock and cider.

3 Bring to the boil slowly and continue to cook, stirring, until thickened. Return the chicken to the pan and adjust the seasoning.

4 Cover the pan and simmer gently for 15 minutes. Turn the chicken pieces over. Re-cover the pan and cook for a further 15 minutes, until the chicken is quite tender.

5 Meanwhile, quarter and core the eating apple, halve each quarter lengthways. Melt the remaining butter in a frying pan and fry until golden but still crisp.

6 Garnish the dish with the fried apple slices.

Casserole of Grouse with Red Wine

❦

This is an ideal way to cook older grouse when the flesh may be slightly dry or tough. Their flavour seeps into the cooking juices to give a rich, gamey taste.

❦

Serves Four

2 brace grouse
45 ml (3 tbsp) polyunsaturated oil plus a little extra
450 g (1 lb) shallots or button onions, skinned
4 large celery sticks, trimmed and sliced
200 ml (7 fl oz) red wine
2 bay leaves
salt and freshly ground pepper
200 ml (7 fl oz) stock
15–20 ml (3–4 tsp) arrowroot
15 ml (1 tbsp) lemon juice
chopped parsley, to garnish

❦

1 Wipe the grouse, trim feet and remove any feather ends. Heat 45 ml (3 tbsp) oil in a large frying pan and brown the birds well; then lift out of the pan.

2 Add the shallots and celery to the pan with a little extra oil if necessary and lightly brown. Transfer the grouse to a casserole dish.

3 Pour the wine into the pan and bring to the boil. Add bay leaves and seasoning and pour over the grouse.

4 Cover and bake at 170°C (325°F) mark 3 for about 50 minutes, or until the grouse are just tender. Lift the birds out of the juice; keep warm, covered.

5 Add stock to the casserole and warm slightly. Mix the arrowroot to a smooth paste with a little water and add to the pan ingredients. Bring to the boil, stirring, and cook until slightly thickened. Stir in the lemon juice, adjust seasoning and spoon over the birds. Garnish with parsley.

Duckling with Green Peas

❧

This particular recipe for the well-known combination of duckling and green peas is much less fatty than some. Use a fresh, free-range duckling for the best results. If fresh peas are not available, frozen ones can be substituted. There is no need to blanch them.

❧

Serves Four–Five
2–2.3 kg (4½–5 lb) duckling
40 g (1½ oz) butter
12–15 pickling or small onions, skinned
450 g (1 lb) shelled peas
50 g (2 oz) smoked streaky bacon, diced
60 ml (4 tbsp) veal stock
2 summer savory sprigs
salt and freshly ground pepper

1 Prick the skin of the duck, taking care not to pierce the flesh. Place on a rack in a roasting tin and cook at 220°C (425°F) mark 7 for 40 minutes.

2 Melt the butter in a saucepan, add the onions and cook, turning frequently, until lightly browned. Blanch peas for 3 minutes, refresh and drain well. Blanch the bacon for 1 minute, rinse and drain well.

3 Pour the surplus fat from the roasting tin then stir the stock into the sediment. Mix the peas, bacon, onions and savory together, place around the duck, season the duck and vegetables and cook at 170°C (325°F) mark 3 for about 20–30 minutes until the duck is cooked and the juices run clear when the thickest part of the leg is pierced with a fine skewer.

4 Serve the duck surrounded by the vegetables and with the cooking juices.

Casseroled Pigeons with Cider and Apple

The cider and apples give this casserole a delicious fruity taste.

❧

Serves Four

3 medium carrots, pealed

3 celery sticks

4 small eating apples

4 pigeons oven-ready

salt and pepper

45 ml (3 tbsp) vegetable oil

40 g (1½ oz) butter or margarine

1 medium onion, skinned and chopped

450 ml (¾ pint) dry cider

150 ml (¼ pint) chicken stock

sprig of fresh thyme

1 bay leaf

pinch of cayenne pepper

pinch of freshly grated nutmeg

20 ml (4 tsp) redcurrant jelly

Worcestershire sauce, if necessary

watercress sprigs, to garnish

❧

1 Roughly chop one of the carrots, one of the celery sticks and two of the apples.

2 Season the pigeons inside and out with salt and pepper. Heat 30 ml (2 tbsp) of the oil and 25 g (1 oz) of the butter in a large frying pan, add the pigeons and seal evenly on all sides. Remove from the pan and set aside.

3 Add the chopped onion, carrot, celery and apples to the pan and fry for 2 minutes until golden brown. Transfer to a large casserole and place the pigeons on top.

4 Pour the cider and stock into the pan and bring to the boil. Add to the casserole with the thyme, bay leaf, cayenne and nutmeg.

5 Cover the casserole and cook in the oven at 150°C (300°F) mark 2 for 1½–2 hours until the birds are quite tender.

6 Meanwhile, cut the remaining apples in half widthways and scoop out the centre using a melon baller. Place a little redcurrant jelly in the centre of each and arrange on a greased baking tray.

7 Twenty minutes before the end of the cooking time, cook the apples in the oven until tender.

8 Cut the remaining carrots and celery sticks into julienne strips and fry in the remaining oil and butter until just beginning to soften. Keep warm.

9 When the pigeons are cooked, remove from the casserole and keep warm. Strain the juices and vegetables from the casserole through a sieve, pushing the vegetables with the back of a wooden spoon. Pour the strained juices into a saucepan, bring to the boil and cook until a syrupy consistency. Season to taste with salt and pepper and add a dash of Worcestershire sauce if the sauce is too sweet.

10 Serve the pigeons on a pool of the sauce and garnish with the apple halves, julienne vegetables and watercress sprigs.

CASSEROLED PIGEONS WITH CIDER AND APPLE (*opposite*)

Rabbit and Forcemeat Pie

❧

Chicken joints can be used instead of the rabbit in this unusual pie.

❧

Serves Four

4 rabbit portions, total weight 550 g (1¼ lb)

30 ml (2 tbsp) plain flour

25 g (1 oz) lard

225 g (8 oz) button onions, skinned and quartered

225 g (8 oz) button mushrooms, trimmed

1 garlic clove, skinned and crushed

100 ml (4 fl oz) port

300 ml (½ pint) chicken stock

12 juniper berries, crushed

350 g (12 oz) sausage meat

45 ml (3 tbsp) chopped fresh parsley

30 ml (2 tbsp) prepared English mustard

225 g (8 oz) shortcrust pastry made with 225 g (8 oz) plain flour

❧

1 Toss the rabbit portions in the flour.

2 Heat the lard in a frying pan and fry the onions, mushrooms and garlic until beginning to brown. Transfer them to a 1.7 litre (3 pint) pie dish.

3 Add the rabbit portions and fry until browned, then transfer to the pie dish. Stir the port, stock and juniper berries into the pan. Bring to the boil, scraping sediment from the base. Add to dish.

4 Mix together the sausage meat, parsley, mustard and seasoning. Shape into 8 balls. Add to pie dish.

5 Roll out the pastry to 5 cm (2 in) wider than the top of the dish. Cut a 2.5 cm (1 in) strip and use to line the dampened rim of the dish. Cover with the pastry lid. Make a hole in the centre.

6 Bake in the oven at 190°C (375°F) mark 5 for 30 minutes. Cover with foil. Reduce temperature to 180°C (350°F) mark 4 for a further 1 hour.

Roast Duck with Pecan and Orange Stuffing

❧

This fragrant stuffing perfectly complements the duck.

❧

Serves Four

2 kg (4 lb) duck

15 ml (1 tbsp) plain flour

600 ml (1 pint) duck stock

STUFFING

75 g (3 oz) dried apricots, chopped

100 ml (4 fl oz) fresh orange juice

40 g (1½ oz) butter

1 small onion, skinned and finely chopped

1 celery stick, trimmed and chopped

the duck liver, chopped

225 g (8 oz) pork sausage meat

50 g (2 oz) fresh breadcrumbs

75 g (3 oz) chopped pecan nuts

1 egg

finely grated rind of 1 orange

15 ml (1 tbsp) brandy

15 ml (1 tbsp) chopped parsley

1.25 ml (¼ tsp) dried thyme

1 To make the stuffing, soak the dried apricots in half the orange juice for 1 hour, then drain and finely chop. Melt the butter and fry the onion and celery until soft. Add the duck liver and cook for 2 minutes. Mix all the remaining ingredients together in a large bowl then add the liver mixture. Allow to cool slightly. Wash the duck and dry it completely with absorbent kitchen paper. Spoon the stuffing into the neck end of the duck and truss.

2 Put the duck on a wire rack in a roasting tin and sprinkle the breast liberally with salt and pepper. Rub the seasoning thoroughly into the skin. Prick the skin all over with a fork or skewer to allow the fat to escape. Roast at 190°C (375°F) mark 5, allowing 20 minutes per 500 g (1 lb), basting occasionally with the fat in the tin. While the duck is cooking, bring the stock to the boil in a saucepan and boil rapidly until reduced to about 300 ml (½ pint). Cool and skim the fat off the surface of the liquid.

3 The duck is cooked when a skewer pushed into the thigh releases clear, not pink, juices. Transfer to a warm dish, remove the trussing string and keep hot.

4 Drain the fat from the roasting tin and stir the flour into the remaining juices. Bring to the boil, stirring constantly to prevent it sticking. Gradually stir in the reduced stock and the remaining orange juice. Cook the gravy for about 10 minutes, stirring, until smooth and thickened. Season to taste and serve with the duck.

Jugged Hare

Order the hare a few days in advance and remember to ask for the blood.

75 ml (5 level tbsp) seasoned flour
125 g (4 oz) streaky bacon, rinded and diced
50 g (2 oz) butter or margarine
900 ml (1½ pints) beef stock
150 ml (¼ pint) port
5 ml (1 level tsp) dried marjoram
45 ml (3 level tbsp) redcurrant jelly
2 medium onions, skinned and stuck with 12 cloves
chopped fresh parsley, to garnish

1 Wipe the hare and toss in the seasoned flour.

2 Brown the bacon in its own fat in a large frying pan then transfer to a casserole.

3 Add the butter to the pan and lightly brown the hare portions. Transfer to the casserole. Add the stock, port, marjoram, redcurrant jelly, onions and seasoning to the pan.

4 Bring to the boil, pour into the casserole, cover and cook at 170°C (325°F) mark 3 for 3 hours.

5 Transfer the hare to a deep serving dish, cover and keep warm. Discard onions.

6 Pour the cooking juices into a saucepan. Mix the blood with juices until smooth. Heat gently, adjust seasoning and pour over hare. Garnish with chopped parsley.

Pheasant Breasts with Vermouth

Ask your butcher to prepare the pheasant fillets used here for you.

Serves Four

1 brace pheasants
30 ml (2 tbsp) plain flour
salt and freshly ground pepper
30 ml (2 tbsp) polyunsaturated oil
50 g (2 oz) onion, skinned and finely chopped
150 ml (¼ pint) dry vermouth
150 ml (¼ pint) chicken stock
30 ml (2 tbsp) chopped fresh sage or 5 ml (1 tsp) dried
30 ml (2 tbsp) single cream
175 g (6 oz) white grapes, preferably seedless
fresh sage leaves and pared courgette strips, to serve

1 Using a sharp knife cut all the breast flesh off the bone, keeping each fillet in one piece. You will end up with 4 breast fillets, 2 from each bird. Use the legs and carcass for a casserole. Ease off the skin and trim away any fat.

2 Dip the fillets in seasoned flour and then brown well in the oil in a medium-sized sauté pan. Remove from the pan using draining spoons.

3 Add the onion with any remaining flour and cook, stirring, for 1–2 minutes. Blend in the vermouth, stock, sage and seasoning. Bring to the boil, stirring, then return pheasant to the pan.

4 Cover tightly and simmer for about 30 minutes, turning once. Lift the pheasant out of the juices and place on a serving dish. Keep warm, covered.

5 Stir the cream and halved grapes (pipped if necessary) into the juices and simmer for 1 minute. Adjust seasoning. Spoon over the pheasant and garnish with sage leaves and pared courgette strips.

Rabbit in the Dairy

This is a sympathetic method of cooking young rabbit that works equally well with chicken joints. It is pale, but is deliberately left ungarnished so as not to detract from the delicate flavour. Instead, serve it on a colourful plate. Young broad beans and new potatoes cooked in their skins are good accompaniments.

Serves Four

1 small celery stick, trimmed and finely chopped
1 shallot, skinned and finely chopped
25 g (1 oz) cooked ham, finely chopped
1 young rabbit, jointed
salt and white pepper
2 fresh bay leaves
300 ml (½ pint) milk

1 Arrange the celery, shallot and ham in a heavy earthenware casserole. Place the pieces of rabbit on top, season and add the bay leaves.

2 Bring the milk to the boil and pour over the rabbit. Cover tightly and cook at 170°C (325°F) mark 3 for about 2 hours until the rabbit is tender.

3 Strain off the cooking liquid and boil to reduce slightly. Taste and adjust the seasoning. Transfer the rabbit, vegetables and ham to a warmed serving plate or dish and pour the liquid over.

PHEASANT BREASTS WITH VERMOUTH (*opposite*)

Michaelmas Goose

❧

Queen Elizabeth I ordered that roast goose should be served in commemoration of the defeat of the Spanish Armada on Michaelmas Day. A Michaelmas goose, fattened on the gleanings from the cornfields, was less fatty than a Christmas bird. It was customarily served with other foods available at the same time – the first wind-fall apples and Fermenty pudding made from the new corn.

❧

Serves Six–Eight

3.5–4.5 kg (8–10 lb) goose, trussed weight
salt and freshly ground pepper

STUFFING

50 g (2 oz) butter
2 onions, skinned and finely chopped
the goose liver, finely chopped
45 ml (3 tbsp) finely chopped fresh sage
175 g (6 oz) fresh white breadcrumbs
finely grated rind and juice of 1 lemon

SAUCE

450 g (1 lb) cooking apples
25 g (1 oz) unsalted butter
25–50 g (1–2 oz) sugar
2 cloves or a pinch of freshly grated nutmeg

❧

1 To make the stuffing, melt the butter, add the onions and cook gently, stirring occasionally, until softened but not browned. Stir in the liver and cook until it just begins to stiffen and change colour. Remove from the heat and stir in the sage,

breadcrumbs, lemon rind and juice and seasoning.

2 Remove any lumps of fat from the cavity of the goose, then season it well inside and out. Spoon the stuffing into the neck end. Do not pack the stuffing too tightly. If there is too much stuffing, put the extra in a roasting tin and cook in the oven 30 minutes before the end of the cooking time.

3 Truss the goose neatly, then prick the breasts, sides and legs. Place the bird, breast side up, on a rack in a roasting tin and cook at 220°C (425°F) mark 7 for 20 minutes.

4 Turn the goose over. Reduce the temperature to 170°C (325°F) mark 3 and cook for 1 hour. Turn the goose over again on to its back and cook for about 1 hour until the juices run clear when the thickest part of the leg is pierced with a skewer. Pour off the fat several times during the cooking.

5 Meanwhile, make the apple sauce. Put the apples, butter, sugar, cloves or nutmeg and 15 ml (1 tbsp) water in a saucepan, cover and cook gently until soft. Beat to a smooth purée.

6 Leave the goose to stand in a warm place for 15 minutes before carving. Serve with the apple sauce.

Side Dishes

Steamed Broccoli with Lemon Sauce

✦

Steaming the broccoli helps to retain the shape of the delicate heads. Serve with steamed fish fillets or crisp fish cakes or croquettes.

✦

Serves Six
900 g (2 lb) broccoli
1 lemon
25 g (1 oz) polyunsaturated margarine
15 ml (1 tbsp) plain flour
salt and freshly ground pepper
lemon slices, to garnish

1 Trim the broccoli, reserving any coarse stalks. Place in a metal colander and cover tightly with foil.
2 Roughly chop the stalks and place in a saucepan of boiling water with a few lemon slices.
3 Place the colander over a saucepan and steam for about 12 minutes, or until the broccoli is just tender. Remove the colander and keep the broccoli warm. Strain the cooking liquor.
4 Melt the margarine in a saucepan, add the flour and cook, stirring, for 1–2 minutes. Stir in 300 ml (½ pint) reserved liquor. Bring to the boil and boil until thickened; season.
5 Pour the sauce into a blender or food processor, add 175 g (6 oz) cooked broccoli and whirl until almost smooth. Return to the saucepan to reheat.
6 Split the broccoli into small florets and serve on a puddle of sauce garnished with lemon slices.

STEAMED BROCCOLI WITH LEMON SAUCE (*page 53*)

LEEKS AU GRATIN (*page 56*)

Leeks au Gratin

The mustard and Cheddar cheese give a bite to this robust winter dish, which is excellent served with gammon or pork.

Serves Four

4 medium leeks, trimmed
salt and freshly ground pepper
25 g (1 oz) butter or margarine
45 ml (3 tbsp) plain flour
300 ml (½ pint) milk
2.5 ml (½ tsp) mustard powder
100 g (4 oz) Cheddar cheese, grated
50 g (2 oz) fresh breadcrumbs

1 Remove the outer leaves of the leeks. Cut each leek in half lengthways and wash thoroughly under running cold water. Cook in boiling salted water for 10–15 minutes and drain thoroughly.

2 Melt the butter in a saucepan, stir in the flour and cook gently for 1 minute, stirring. Remove the pan from the heat and gradually stir in the milk. Bring to the boil slowly and continue to cook, stirring, until the sauce thickens. Stir in the seasoning, mustard and half the cheese.

3 Arrange the leeks in a greased baking dish and pour over the cheese sauce.

4 Mix together the remaining cheese and breadcrumbs and spoon over the dish. Brown under a hot grill or in the oven.

Garlicky Sliced Potatoes

Make sure you use old potatoes for this dish, which makes an excellent accompaniment to roast meats or casseroles.

1.4 kg (3 lb) old potatoes
40 g (1½ oz) polyunsaturated margarine
salt and freshly ground pepper
1 garlic clove, skinned and crushed
450 ml (¾ pint) milk

1 Peel and thinly slice the potatoes. Arrange them in overlapping layers in a shallow, greased, 1.8 litre (3¼ pint) ovenproof dish, seasoning well between each layer.

2 Add the crushed garlic to the milk, stir well then pour over the potatoes. Dot the surface with the remaining margarine.

3 Stand the dish on a baking sheet. Cook at 200°C (400°F) mark 6 for about 45 minutes, increase to 220°C (425°F) mark 7 and bake for a further 30 minutes or until the sliced potatoes are tender when tested and golden brown and the seasoned milk has been absorbed.

Creamed Mushrooms

*These creamy mushrooms on toast are perfect for a
quick supper or light lunch.*

Serves Four

25 g (1 oz) butter or margarine
450 g (1 lb) button mushrooms, sliced
20 ml (4 tsp) cornflour
150 ml (¼ pint) milk
60 ml (4 tbsp) single cream
salt and freshly ground pepper
4 large slices of bread
butter or margarine, for spreading

1 Melt the butter in a saucepan, add the mushrooms and sauté gently for 5 minutes.
2 Blend the cornflour to a smooth paste with a
little of the milk. Stir into the remaining milk, then
add to the pan. Bring to the boil, stirring, and cook
for 1–2 minutes, until the sauce thickens.
3 Mix in the cream and seasoning, and reheat
without boiling. Toast the bread and spread with
butter. Pile the creamed mixture on top.

Turnips in Mustard Sauce

*Equally as good served with roast beef or mackerel,
this dish has a definite bite to it. If available, use
whole baby turnips as they are deliciously sweet.*

Serves Four–Six

1 kg (2¼ lb) turnips, peeled and cut into pieces
450 ml (¾ pint) chicken stock
25 g (1 oz) butter or margarine
45 ml (3 tbsp) plain flour
300 ml (½ pint) milk
15 ml (1 tbsp) mustard powder
10 ml (2 tsp) sugar
15 ml (1 tbsp) vinegar
salt and freshly ground pepper

1 Put the turnip pieces in a saucepan and add the
stock. Cover, bring to the boil and cook for about
30 minutes, until tender.
2 Meanwhile, make the sauce: melt the butter in a
pan, stir in the flour and cook gently for 1 minute,
stirring. Remove pan from the heat and gradually
stir in the milk. Bring to the boil slowly and continue to cook, stirring, until the sauce thickens.
3 Blend the mustard and sugar with the vinegar,
add to the sauce and reheat. Drain the turnips, add
to the mustard sauce, season and reheat gently.

LEFT TO RIGHT: BRAISED CARROTS AND CELERY (*page 60*); TURNIPS IN MUSTARD SAUCE (*page 57*)

LEFT TO RIGHT: GLAZED SHALLOTS (*page 60*); CELERIAC AND ONION BAKE (*page 61*)

Glazed Shallots

The light sugar glaze in this recipe enhances the shallots' mild taste.

Serves Four

450 g (1 lb) shallots, skinned
50 g (2 oz) butter
10 ml (2 tbsp) sugar
salt and freshly ground pepper
chopped fresh parsley, to garnish

1 Place the shallots in a pan and cover with cold water. Bring to the boil and blanch for 10 minutes. Drain.

2 Melt the butter in a saucepan, add the sugar, shallots and salt and pepper. Cover and cook for about 15 minutes, until the shallots are tender and well glazed. Stir occasionally to prevent the sugar from burning. Turn into a warmed serving dish and sprinkle with parsley.

Braised Carrots and Celery

Serve this recipe with a robust grilled fish such as mackerel or cod.

Serves Six

450 g (1 lb) carrots
1 head celery
25 g (1 oz) polyunsaturated margarine
salt and freshly ground pepper
300 ml (½ pint) unsweetened apple juice
chopped fresh parsley, to garnish

1 Pare the carrots and cut into even sized pieces. Trim and cut the celery into 4 cm (1½ in) pieces.

2 Heat the margarine in a large saucepan, add the carrots and cook, stirring, for 2–3 minutes. Add the celery and cook for a further minute. Season.

3 Pour over the apple juice, cover and simmer for about 20 minutes, or until the vegetables are barely tender. Uncover and bubble down the juices to reduce slightly; shake the pan occasionally.

4 Adjust seasoning for serving and garnish with chopped parsley.

Celeriac and Onion Bake

When buying celeriac, choose a root that feels heavy and is unblemished. This flavoursome bake is an excellent accompaniment to game.

Serves Four

900 g (2 lb) celeriac, peeled and cut into 0.5 cm (¼ in) slices
1 large onion, skinned and thinly sliced
salt and freshly ground pepper
50 g (2 oz) butter or margarine
150 ml (¼ pint) milk

1 Layer the celeriac and onion slices in a greased ovenproof dish. Sprinkle each layer with seasoning and dot with butter.
2 Pour over the milk and cook, uncovered, in the oven at 190°C (375°F) mark 5 for about 1¼ hours, until the celeriac is soft and golden brown on top.

Gingered Beetroot

A spicy dish that is the perfect accompaniment for roasted chicken or turkey.

Serves Four

450 g (1 lb) beetroot
25 g (1 oz) butter
25 g (1 oz) crystallised ginger, finely chopped
2 pineapple slices, chopped
45 ml (3 tbsp) white wine vinegar
30 ml (2 tbsp) sugar
salt and freshly ground pepper

1 Trim the stalks to within 2.5 cm (1 in) of the beetroot and leave whole. Cook in boiling salted water for 1–3 hours, according to size. The skin will rub off easily when cooked. Drain well, peel and cut into 0.5 cm (¼ in) dice.
2 Melt the butter in a large saucepan, add the beetroot, ginger, pineapple, vinegar, sugar and seasoning. Heat through, stirring, before serving.

Puddings

Raspberry Soufflé

❧

Frozen raspberries may be used when fresh ones are not available. Other purées, such as strawberry, apricot, blackberry, blackcurrant, blueberry or mango, may be used instead of raspberry.

❧

Serves Six–Eight

700 g (1½ lb) raspberries

6 eggs, separated

100 g (4 oz) caster sugar

30 ml (2 tbsp) powdered gelatine

600 ml (1 pint) whipping cream

DECORATION

150 ml (¼ pint) double cream, whipped

fresh raspberries

1 Prepare a 20.5 cm (8 in) soufflé dish with a greaseproof paper collar. Press the raspberries through a nylon sieve to make a purée.

2 Whisk the egg yolks and sugar in a large bowl, until pale and thick and the mixture holds the trail of a whisk for at least 5 seconds. Whisk in the purée.

3 Sprinkle the gelatine over 90 ml (6 tbsp) water in a small bowl and leave to soften for 2 minutes. Stand in a saucepan of hot water and stir until dissolved and very hot.

4 Whip the cream until it will hold soft peaks. Whisk the egg whites until stiff, but not dry.

5 Whisk the gelatine into the raspberry mixture. Fold in the cream, then the egg whites. Pour the mixture into the prepared soufflé dish and level the surface. Chill until set.

6 Carefully peel off the paper from the soufflé. Decorate the top of the soufflé with piped cream and fresh raspberries.

RASPBERRY SOUFFLE (*opposite*)

Wine and Pear Jelly

❧

Homemade wine jelly has long been a family favourite.

❧

Serves Six
450 ml (¾ pint) red wine
50 g (2 oz) caster sugar
2 cinnamon sticks
6 green cardamoms
6 medium-sized ripe pears
20 ml (4 tsp) powdered gelatine
30 ml (2 tbsp) lemon juice
whipped cream, to serve
toasted shredded coconut, to decorate

❧

1 Place the wine in a medium-sized saucepan with 450 ml (¾ pint) water. Add the sugar, cinnamon sticks and cardamoms and heat gently until the sugar dissolves. Boil for 1–2 minutes.
2 Peel, quarter and core the pears. Poach gently in the wine syrup until tender (about 20 minutes). Lift the pears carefully out of the syrup; cool.
3 Spoon 60 ml (4 tbsp) water into a small bowl. Sprinkle over the gelatine and leave to soak for about 10 minutes. Dissolve by standing the bowl in a pan of simmering water.
4 Stir the dissolved gelatine into the strained syrup. Add the lemon juice and cool.
5 Spoon a thin layer of jelly into a 1.4 litre (2½ pint) ring mould. Top with a ring of pears. Chill until set. Continue layering up jelly and pears until the mould is full. Refrigerate to firm up.

6 Turn out the jelly, decorate with the coconut and serve with lightly whipped cream.

Blackberry Mousses

❧

This mousse is made without gelatine and must be chilled thoroughly before serving. It can also be made with raspberries or strawberries.

❧

Serves Six
225 g (8 oz) blackberries, fresh or frozen
2 eggs, separated
50 g (2 oz) caster sugar
300 ml (½ pint) double cream
a few blackberries, with leaves if possible, to decorate

❧

1 Press the blackberries through a nylon sieve to make a purée (about 225 ml 8 fl oz).
2 Whisk the egg yolks in a large mixing bowl with the caster sugar until very thick, then whisk in the blackberry purée.
3 Whip the cream until thick enough to leave a trail on the surface when the whisk is lifted, then fold into the blackberry mixture. Continue to whisk until the mixture will form a heavy trail. Whisk the egg whites until they stand in soft peaks, then fold into the blackberry mixture.
4 Spoon the blackberry mousse into 6 ramekins and chill for about 2 hours. Serve decorated with fresh blackberries and their leaves, hung in clusters over the sides.

Fruit Crumble

❧

Fruit crumbles are high on the list of favourite English puddings. They are extremely simple to make and any type of fruit that grows wild or in the garden can be used.

❧

Serves Four

700 g (1 ½ lb) raw fruit, such as blackberries, apples, plums, rhubarb, prepared and sliced according to type
100–175 g (4–6 oz) caster sugar
100 g (4 oz) plain flour
pinch of salt
50 g (2 oz) hard butter or margarine, chopped
50 g (2 oz) Demerara sugar
custard, to serve

❧

1 Put the fruit into a buttered ovenproof dish and add caster sugar to taste.
2 Sift the flour and salt together, toss in the butter or margarine, then rub the fat in until the mixture resembles breadcrumbs. Stir in the Demerara sugar.
3 Spoon the crumble over the fruit and bake at 190°C (375°F) mark 5 for 25–30 minutes until the top is brown and the fruit tender. Serve with custard.

Pears Cooked in Red Wine

❧

Once cooked, the pears will keep very well in a refrigerator for up to a week – improving in flavour as the wine penetrates deeper into them. Always make at least one day before serving.

❧

Serves Six–Eight

70 cl bottle of red wine
175 g (6 oz) granulated sugar
strained juice of 1 large orange
strained juice of 1 large lemon
10 cm (4 in) piece of cinnamon stick
6 allspice
6–8 large ripe, but firm, pears
lightly whipped cream, to serve

❧

1 Put the red wine into a large stainless steel saucepan with the sugar, orange and lemon juice, and the spices. Heat gently until the sugar has dissolved, then bring to the boil and boil for 1 minute.
2 Carefully peel the pears, leaving their stalks on. Put the pears into the spiced wine. Cover and cook gently until the pears are just tender when pierced with the tip of a knife. Turn the pears frequently during cooking.
3 Using a slotted spoon, transfer the pears to a serving bowl and set aside. Bring the wine to the boil, then boil gently until it is reduced by about half. Pour the reduced wine over the pears, allow to cool, then cover and chill. Serve with lightly whipped cream.

BLACKBERRY MOUSSE (*page 64*)

ORANGES COOKED IN CARAMEL (*page 68*)

Oranges Cooked in Caramel

Although they are an old favourite, oranges cooked in caramel are still a very popular dessert. Serve with crème Chantilly.

Serves Six
225 g (8 oz) granulated sugar
300 ml (½ pint) boiling water
6 large oranges
30–45 ml (2–3 tbsp) Grand Marnier
double cream, to serve

1 Put the sugar into a saucepan with 50 ml (2 fl oz) cold water and heat gently until the sugar has dissolved, brushing down the sides of the saucepan with hot water. Bring to the boil, then boil until the syrup turns a golden caramel colour.

2 Immediately, plunge the base of the saucepan into cold water to prevent the caramel darkening further. Carefully pour the boiling water into the pan. Return the caramel to the heat, and heat gently until it has completely dissolved into the water.

3 Meanwhile, thinly pare the rind from two of the oranges, taking care not to remove the white pith. Cut the rind into very fine shreds and set aside. Using a very sharp knife, remove the skin and white pith from all the oranges.

4 Put the oranges and the shredded rinds into the caramel, cover and cook them very gently for 25–30 minutes until the oranges are tender, but do not allow to overcook – they must retain a good shape. Turn the oranges frequently during cooking.

5 Transfer the oranges and their syrup to a large serving dish. Add the Grand Marnier, and allow to cool. Cover and chill.

Minted Strawberry Custards

Replace the mint with a few lemon geranium leaves if you wish.

Serves Six
450 ml (¾ pint) milk
4 large mint sprigs, rinsed
1 egg
2 egg yolks
45 ml (3 tbsp) caster sugar
20 ml (4 tsp) powdered gelatine
700 g (1½ lb) fresh strawberries
polyunsaturated oil
15 ml (1 tbsp) icing sugar
fresh strawberries, to decorate

1 Place the milk and mint sprigs in a saucepan. Bring slowly to the boil, cover and leave to infuse for about 30 minutes.

2 Whisk the whole egg and the yolks with the caster sugar. Strain over the milk. Return to the pan and cook gently, stirring, until the custard just coats the back of the spoon. Do *not* boil. Cool.

3 Dissolve the gelatine in 45 ml (3 tbsp) water following manufacturer's instructions. Stir into the custard.

4 Purée and sieve the strawberries. Whisk about two-thirds into the cold, but not set, custard.

5 Oil six 150 ml (¼ pint) ramekin dishes. Pour in the custard and refrigerate to set (about 3 hours).

6 Meanwhile, whisk the icing sugar into the remaining strawberry purée, refrigerate.

7 To serve, turn out the custards. Surround with strawberry sauce; decorate with strawberries.

Bakewell Tart

As with many traditional dishes there are a number of different recipes that are claimed as the genuine, authentic one. In the case of this dish, there is also a dispute about whether it should be called a tart or pudding. The ground almonds in this particularly delicious version can be replaced in part or completely by flour.

Serves Four–Six

shortcrust pastry, made with 100 g (4 oz) plain flour
50 g (2 oz) unsalted butter
50 g (2 oz) caster sugar
1 ½ eggs, beaten
100 g (4 oz) ground almonds
raspberry jam
icing sugar, for sifting

1 Roll out the pastry on a lightly floured surface and use to line a 15 cm (6 in) flan dish placed on a baking sheet. Chill for 30 minutes.

2 Prick the base lightly, cover with greaseproof paper and scatter a layer of baking beans over the paper. Bake blind at 200°C (400°F) mark 6 for 10 minutes. Remove the baking beans and greaseproof lining paper and return the pastry to the oven for a further 5 minutes.

3 Meanwhile, beat the butter and sugar together in a bowl until light and fluffy, then gradually beat in the eggs, beating well after each addition. Fold in the almonds.

4 Spread a thin layer of jam over the base of the pastry case. Fill with the almond mixture. Bake for about 25 minutes until the filling is just firm.

5 Sift icing sugar over the top. Serve warm or cold.

SUMMER PUDDING (*page 72*)

STRAWBERRY FLAN (*page 73*)

Summer Pudding

Summer Pudding was created in the eighteenth century as an alternative to the rich crusty pastry desserts that were then fashionable. Any combination of mixed summer red berries and currants can be used.

Serves Six

900 g (2 lb) of a mixture of any of the following:
blackcurrants, redcurrants, raspberries, loganberries,
strawberries, blackberries
about 150 g (5 oz) caster sugar
about 8 thin slices of bread, crusts removed
cream, or plain yogurt, to serve

1 Put the fruit in a bowl, sprinkle the sugar over, cover and leave overnight. Put the fruit and juice into a saucepan, then heat gently for 2–3 minutes. Taste and add more sugar if necessary.

2 Cut some of the bread into wedge shapes to fit into the bottom of a 1.1 litre (2 pint) pudding basin. Cut and arrange the remaining bread so that it lines the bowl neatly with no spaces between the slices.

3 Fill with the fruit and most of the juice, then cover the fruit completely with a layer of bread. Spoon the remaining juice over the top layer of bread. Place a plate that just fits inside the basin on top of the pudding. Put one or more weights on top and leave in a cool place overnight.

4 To serve, carefully run a knife between the pudding and the bowl, then invert on to a serving plate. Serve with cream or plain yogurt.

Winter Compôte

A compote with a bitter sweet flavour, tangy and refreshing.

Serves Six–Eight

basic sugar syrup
450 g (1 lb) kumquats, thickly sliced
450 g (1 lb) clementines, peeled and segmented
175 g (6 oz) black grapes
175 g (6 oz) green grapes
175 g (6 oz) cranberries

1 Make the sugar syrup in a wide saucepan. Add the kumquats, cover and cook gently for about 15–20 minutes until barely tender.

2 Add the clementines and grapes, then cook for a further 5 minutes, gently turning the fruits in the syrup and taking care not to break them up. Add the cranberries and cook for about 5 minutes until softened.

3 Carefully transfer the fruits and syrup to a serving bowl. Serve hot or cold.

Strawberry Flan

❧

This classic French strawberry flan is simplicity itself, but you must use full-flavoured strawberries and a good strawberry conserve to produce the best results.

❧

Serves Eight
1 quantity of almond pastry (next recipe)
500 g (1 lb 2 oz) strawberry conserve
45 ml (3 tbsp) Cointreau
700 g (1 ½ lb) fresh strawberries, hulled
lightly whipped cream, to serve

❧

1 Roll out the almond pastry on a lightly floured surface to a round 2.5 cm (1 in) larger than a 25 cm (10 in) flan dish. Line the dish with the pastry. Trim the edges, then prick the pastry all over. Chill for at least 30 minutes, then bake at 220°C (425°F) mark 7 for 25–30 minutes until very lightly browned. Allow to cool.

2 Put the strawberry conserve into a saucepan, heat gently until melted, then sieve through a nylon sieve into another clean saucepan. Stir in the Cointreau and bring to the boil.

3 Brush a little of the strawberry glaze over the bottom and up the sides of the flan case. Arrange the strawberries, pointed ends up, neatly in the flan case.

4 Spoon the remaining strawberry glaze over the strawberries until they are all evenly coated. Serve with lightly whipped cream.

Almond Pastry

❧

Almond pastry is very similar to pâte sucrée, and is also used for flan and tartlet cases. Because it has the addition of the ground almonds, it is a very soft pastry to handle and must be chilled before using.

❧

Makes about 400g (14oz)
150 g (5 oz) plain flour
pinch of salt
40 g (1 ½ oz) caster sugar
50 g (2 oz) ground almonds
90 g (3 ½ oz) butter, cubed
few drops of vanilla essence
1 egg, beaten

❧

1 Sift the flour, salt and sugar into a bowl, then mix in the ground almonds. Rub in the butter until the mixture resembles fine breadcrumbs.

2 Make a well in the centre, add the vanilla and the beaten egg. Mix together with a round-bladed knife to form a dough.

3 Turn on to a lightly floured surface and knead for a few seconds until smooth.

4 Wrap the pastry in greaseproof paper and chill for 30–40 minutes until firm, before using.

Cakes and Baking

Traditional English Muffins

To serve muffins, pull them almost apart through the centre, toast them and spread with butter. Close them up and eat while still warm.

Makes about Fourteen

5 ml (1 tsp) caster sugar
300 ml (½ pint) warm milk
10 ml (2 tsp) dried yeast
450 g (1 lb) strong white flour
5 ml (1 tsp) salt
5 ml (1 tsp) plain flour, for dusting
5 ml (1 tsp) fine semolina

1 Dissolve the sugar in the milk, sprinkle the yeast over the surface and leave in a warm place for about 20 minutes until frothy.

2 Sift the flour and salt together, then form a well in the centre. Pour the yeast liquid into the well, draw in the flour and mix to a smooth dough.

3 Knead the dough on a lightly floured surface for about 10 minutes until smooth and elastic. Place in a clean bowl, cover with a tea towel and leave in a warm place until doubled in size.

4 Roll out the dough on a lightly floured surface using a lightly floured rolling pin to about 0.5–1 cm (¼–½ in) thick. Leave to rest, covered, for 5 minutes, then cut into rounds with a 7.5 cm (3 in) plain cutter.

5 Place the muffins on a well-floured baking sheet. Mix together the flour and semolina and use to dust the tops. Cover with a tea towel and leave in a warm place until doubled in size.

6 Grease a griddle, electric griddle plate or heavy frying pan and heat over a moderate heat, until a cube of bread turns brown in 20 seconds.

7 Cook the muffins on the griddle or frying pan for about 7 minutes each side.

TRADITIONAL ENGLISH MUFFINS (*opposite*)

Marmalade Spice Cake

This is a moist cake with an unusual crunchy topping.

175 g (6 oz) butter or block margarine
120 ml (8 tbsp) golden syrup
2 large eggs, beaten
150 ml (10 level tbsp) medium-cut orange marmalade
350 g (12 oz) self-raising flour
5 ml (1 tsp) *each* of baking powder, ground nutmeg and
ground cinnamon
1.25 ml (¼ tsp) ground cloves
about 150 ml (¼ pint) milk
50 g (2 oz) cornflakes

1 Grease and base line a 20.5 cm (8 in) square or 23 cm (9 in) round cake tin.
2 Beat the butter – which should be at room temperature – with 90 ml (6 tbsp) of the golden syrup until well mixed. Gradually beat in the eggs keeping the mixture stiff.
3 Chop the marmalade and stir half into the cake mixture.
4 Mix in the flour sifted with the baking powder and spices, adding sufficient milk to give a fairly stiff consistency.
5 Turn into prepared cake tin, level the surface.
6 Crush the cornflakes and mix with the remaining syrup and chopped marmalade. Carefully spread over the cake mixture.
7 Bake at 180°C (350°F) mark 4 for about 1 hour. Turn out and cool on a wire rack.

Dorset Apple Cake

This simple, delicious version of apple cake comes from Dorset and is at its best if served still warm, with custard or brandy butter for a pudding, or plain butter for tea or with mid-morning coffee.

Makes Six–Eight Slices
225 g (8 oz) plain flour
7.5 ml (1½ tsp) baking powder
pinch of salt
100 g (4 oz) butter, diced
165 g (5½ oz) soft light brown sugar
175 g (6 oz) cooking apple, peeled, cored and chopped
1 egg, beaten
milk, to mix
2.5 ml (½ tsp) ground cinnamon

1 Grease and line an 18 cm (7 in) round cake tin.
2 Sift the flour, baking powder and salt together. Rub in the butter until mixture resembles crumbs.
3 Stir in 100 g (4 oz) of the sugar, the apple and the egg. Mix to a dough adding a little milk if too stiff.
4 Put into the prepared tin. Mix the remaining sugar with the cinnamon and sprinkle over the top. Bake at 180°C (350°F) mark 4 for about 45–50 minutes until a light golden brown and cooked through.
5 Cool in the tin for 12 minutes, then turn out.

Rich Cherry Cake

❧

This rich and colourful cake makes a perfect teatime treat.

❧

225 g (8 oz) glacé cherries, halved
150 g (5 oz) self-raising flour
50 g (2 oz) plain flour
45 ml (3 tbsp) cornflour
45 ml (3 tbsp) ground almonds
175 g (6 oz) butter or block margarine, softened
175 g (6 oz) caster sugar
3 eggs, beaten
6 sugar cubes
glacé cherries and angelica, to decorate

❧

1 Grease and base line an 18 cm (7 in) round cake tin. Wash the cherries and dry thoroughly. Sift the flours and cornflour together. Stir in the ground almonds and cherries.
2 Cream the butter and sugar until pale and fluffy. Add the eggs, a little at a time, beating well after each addition. Fold in the dry ingredients.
3 Turn the mixture into the tin, making sure the cherries are not grouped together, and hollow the centre slightly.
4 Roughly crush the sugar cubes with a rolling pin and scatter these over the cake.
5 Bake in the oven at 180°C (350°F) mark 4 for 1–1½ hours, until well risen and golden brown. Turn out and cool on a wire rack. Decorate with glacé cherries and angelica before serving.

Choux Pastry

❧

The secret of making light, crisp pastry is to take great care and not be too hasty when adding the beaten eggs. Thorough beating between each addition will ensure perfect results.

❧

65 g (2½ oz) strong white flour
50 g (2 oz) butter or block margarine
2 eggs, lightly beaten (use size 2 when using an electric mixer)

❧

1 Sift the flour on to a plate or piece of paper. Put the fat and 150 ml (¼ pint) water together in a saucepan, heat gently until the fat has melted, then bring to the boil. Remove the pan from the heat. Tip the flour at once into the hot liquid. Beat thoroughly with a wooden spoon.
2 Continue beating the mixture until it is smooth and forms a ball in the centre of the pan (take care not to overheat or the mixture will become fatty). Leave the mixture to cool for a minute or two.
3 Beat in the eggs a little at a time, adding only just enough to give a piping consistency.
4 It is important to beat the mixture vigorously at this stage to trap in as much air as possible. A hand-held electric mixer is ideal for this purpose. Continue beating until the mixture develops an obvious sheen and then use as required.

MARMALADE SPICE CAKE (*page 76*)

RICH CHERRY CAKE (*page 77*)

Parkin

⠿

English parkin recipes originate in the north of the country and always contain oatmeal, syrup and black treacle.

⠿

Makes Twelve Slices
175 g (6 oz) golden syrup
175 g (6 oz) black treacle
50 g (2 oz) lard, diced
50 g (2 oz) butter or margarine, diced
100 g (4 oz) soft brown sugar
225 g (8 oz) plain flour
pinch of salt
10 ml (2 tsp) ground ginger
2.5 ml (½ tsp) ground cinnamon
7.5 ml (1½ tsp) bicarbonate of soda
225 g (8 oz) medium oatmeal
1 egg, lightly beaten
60 ml (4 tbsp) milk

⠿

1 Grease and line a 23 cm (9 in) square tin.
2 Gently warm the syrup and treacle, lard, butter and sugar together in a small saucepan until the treacle and fats have melted and the sugar has dissolved.
3 Sift the flour, salt, spices and bicarbonate of soda together in a bowl and stir in the oatmeal. Form a well in the centre, then add the egg and milk, beaten together.
4 Pour the warm ingredients into the milk, then gradually draw the dry ingredients into the liquid mixture and beat well to give a smooth batter. Pour

into the prepared tin and bake at 180°C (350°F) mark 4 for about 1 hour.
5 Allow to stand for about 2 minutes before turning out on to a wire rack. Leave for 2 minutes then carefully remove the lining paper. Turn the cake the right way up and leave to cool.
6 Store in an airtight tin for 2–3 days before eating.

Honey and Lemon Round

⠿

These tangy buns would be as welcome at breakfast as at teatime.

⠿

Makes Twelve
7.5 ml (1½ tsp) dried yeast
225 ml (8 fl oz) tepid milk
450 g (1 lb) strong white flour
5 ml (1 tsp) salt
50 g (2 oz) butter or block margarine
5 ml (1 tsp) sugar
grated rind of 1 lemon
1 egg, beaten
30 ml (2 tbsp) clear honey

ICING
175 g (6 oz) icing sugar
15 ml (1 tbsp) clear honey
juice of 1 lemon

⠿

1 Grease a 20.5 cm (8 in) cake tin.
2 Sprinkle the yeast into the milk.

3 Sift the flour and salt into a bowl and rub in the fat. Stir in the sugar and lemon rind. Add the egg and yeast liquid and mix to a soft dough.

4 Turn out on to a floured surface and knead for about 10 minutes. Cover the dough with lightly oiled polythene and leave to rise in a warm place until the mixture has doubled in size.

5 Turn the dough on to a lightly floured surface and knead gently. Roll into a rectangle 30.5 × 23 cm (12 × 9 in) and spread with honey. Roll up from the long side and cut into 12 pieces.

6 Place cut side down in the prepared tin and cover with lightly oiled polythene. Leave in a warm place until doubled in siz .

7 Bake at 190°C (375°F) mark 5 for 20–25 minutes. Cool on a wire rack. Blend the icing sugar with the honey and enough lemon juice to mix to a coating consistency and spoon over the buns.

Cider Cake

A succulent, moist cake from Somerset, the cider county. Store the cake in an air-tight container for at least 2 days before eating, but it will keep for much longer.

Makes Eight–Ten Slices
100 g (4 oz) glacé cherries, chopped
100 g (4 oz) currants
100 g (4 oz) sultanas
100 g (4 oz) raisins
150 ml (¼ pint) dry cider
150 g (5 oz) light soft brown sugar
1 egg, beaten
175 g (6 oz) plain flour
25 g (1 oz) cornflour
10 ml (2 tsp) baking powder
pinch of salt

1 Grease a 900 g (2 lb) loaf tin.

2 Put the fruit and the cider in a bowl and leave to soak in a cool place overnight.

3 Stir in the sugar and egg, then sift in the flour, cornflour, baking powder and salt. Mix well together, then transfer to the greased loaf tin. Bake at 170°C (325°F) mark 3 for 2 hours.

4 Leave to cool slightly in the tin, then turn out on to a wire rack and leave to cool.

Crumpets

Serve the crumpets toasted, with butter, or cheese.

Makes about Fifteen
5 ml (1 tsp) caster sugar
750 ml (1 ¼ pints) warm milk
10 ml (2 tsp) dried yeast
450 g (1 lb) plain flour
5 ml (1 tsp) salt
2.5 ml (½ tsp) bicarbonate of soda

1 Dissolve the sugar in 300 ml (½ pint) of the milk, sprinkle the yeast over the surface then leave in a warm place for about 10 minutes until frothy.

2 Sift the flour and salt into a warm bowl and form a well in the centre. Pour half the yeast liquid into the well, then gradually draw the flour into the liquid using a wooden spoon and beat until smooth. Gradually beat in the remaining liquid to give a thin, batter. Beat well, cover with a tea towel and leave in a warm place until doubled in size.

3 Dissolve the bicarbonate of soda in the remaining milk, beat it into the batter well, then leave for 30 minutes.

4 Grease a griddle, electric griddle plate or heavy frying pan and three 9 cm (3½ in) plain metal cutters or crumpet rings.

5 Heat the griddle or pan and the rings over a moderate heat until a cube of bread turns brown in 20 seconds. Pour enough batter into each ring to fill them to a depth of about 1 cm (½ in).

6 Cook for about 4 minutes until the surface is dry and honeycombed with holes. Carefully remove the rings and turn the crumpets over and cook on the other side for 2–3 minutes. Continue until all the batter is used, greasing and heating the griddle and rings before adding the batter.

Chocolate Eclairs

For a variation, these éclairs could be topped with coffee-flavoured glacé icing.

Makes Twelve
1 quantity of choux pastry (see page 77)
300 ml (10 fl oz) double cream
100 g (4 oz) plain chocolate

1 Dampen a baking sheet. Put the choux pastry into a piping bag fitted with a medium plain nozzle and pipe 9 cm (3½ in) long fingers on to the baking sheet. Trim with a wet knife.

2 Bake in the oven at 200°C (400°F) mark 6 for about 35 minutes, until crisp and golden.

3 Make a slit down the side of each bun with a sharp, pointed knife to release the steam, then transfer to a wire rack and leave to cool.

4 Just before serving, whip the double cream until stiff and use it to fill the éclairs.

5 Break the chocolate into a bowl and place over simmering water. Stir until melted.

6 Pour into a wide shallow bowl and draw the filled éclairs across the chocolate's surface.

CHOCOLATE ECLAIRS (*opposite*)

Chelsea Buns

⚓

Yeast fruit buns were a speciality of the old Chelsea Bun House, Grosvenor Row, and are said to have been bought by, or for, King Georges II, III and IV. Serve freshly made and warm.

⚓

Makes Twelve

225 g (8 oz) strong white flour
7.5 ml (1½ tsp) dried yeast
5 ml (1 tsp) caster sugar
100 ml (4 fl oz) warm milk
2.5 ml (½ tsp) salt
25 g (1 oz) butter, diced
1 egg, beaten
75 g (3 oz) sultanas, currants and chopped raisins, mixed
25 g (1 oz) mixed peel, chopped
50 g (2 oz) soft brown sugar
40 g (1½ oz) butter, melted
icing sugar, for glazing

⚓

1 Grease an 18–20.5 cm (7–8 in) square tin. Sift 50 g (2 oz) of the flour into a warm bowl. Stir in the yeast. Dissolve the caster sugar in the milk and stir into the flour and yeast. Leave in a warm place for about 20 minutes until frothy.

2 Sift the remaining flour and salt into a warm bowl, then rub in the diced butter. Form a well in the centre, pour in the yeast mixture and the egg, then draw in the dry ingredients to make a smooth dough.

3 Knead the dough on a lightly floured surface for about 10 minutes until smooth and elastic. Place in a clean bowl, cover with a tea towel and leave to rise for 1¼–2¼ hours until doubled in size. Knead the dough lightly on a floured surface, then roll it out to a large rectangle, about 30×23 cm (12×9 in).

4 Mix the dried fruit, peel and sugar together. Brush the dough with melted butter, then scatter the fruit mixture over the surface, leaving a 2.5 cm (1 in) clear border around the edges.

5 Roll the dough up tightly like a Swiss roll, starting at a long edge. Press the edges together to seal them. Cut the roll into 12 slices.

6 Place the rolls cut side uppermost in the prepared tin. Cover with a clean tea towel and leave in a warm place until doubled in size.

7 Bake at 190°C (350°F) mark 5 for 30 minutes. Blend a little icing sugar with water to make a sugar glaze and brush over the top while still hot. Leave to cool slightly in the tin before turning out.

Preserves

Grapefruit Whisky Marmalade

Marmalade prepared in the food processor isn't as clear as the hand-cut type, but valuable time is saved.

Makes about 1.8 kg (4 lb)

2 large pink grapefruit, about 900 kg (2 lb) in weight

3–4 lemons, about 450 g (1 lb) in weight

450 g (1 lb) Demerara sugar

900 g (2 lb) granulated sugar

75 ml (3 fl oz) whisky

1 Wipe the fruits, halve and squeeze out the juice. Strain into a large preserving pan; reserve the pips.
2 Scoop the pith out of the fruit shells and tie, with the pips, inside a piece of muslin. Add to the pan.
3 Finely slice the fruit skins. Alternatively, process them using the slicing disc; hand-slice any large bits of peel that escape the blade. Add to the preserving pan with 1.8 litres (3 pints) water.
4 Bring to the boil and simmer for about 1¼ hours or until the peel is quite tender and the contents of the pan reduced by half. Discard the muslin bag.
5 Add the sugars and heat gently until dissolved.

Bring to the boil and boil rapidly for 10–15 minutes or until the setting point is reached. To test for setting point, drop a tiny amount of the marmalade on to a cold saucer, leave to cool, then push the marmalade with a finger. If the surface of the marmalade wrinkles, the setting point has been reached. Remove the pan from the heat while carrying out the test.
6 Skim the marmalade, leave to stand for about 15 minutes and stir in the whisky. Pour into warm, sterilised jars, and put waxed discs, wax side down, on the surface of the marmalade. Cover immediately with a dampened round of cellophane. Store in a cool place.

GRAPEFRUIT WHISKY MARMALADE (*page 85*)

WHOLE STRAWBERRY JAM (*page 88*)

Mint and Apple Jelly

Herb jellies are excellent with hot and cold meat dishes.

2.3 kg (5 lb) cooking apples, chopped
few fresh mint sprigs
1.1 litres (2 pints) distilled vinegar
sugar
90–120 ml (6–8 tbsp) chopped fresh mint
few drops of green food colouring

1 Place the apples in a large saucepan with 1.1 litres (2 pints) water and the mint sprigs. Bring to the boil, then simmer gently for 45 minutes, until the fruit is soft and pulpy. Stir from time to time to pevent sticking. Add the vinegar and boil for a further 5 minutes.
2 Spoon the apple pulp into a jelly bag or cloth attached to the legs of an upturned stool, and leave to strain into a large bowl for at least 12 hours.
3 Discard the pulp remaining in the jelly bag. Measure the juice extract and put it in a preserving pan with 450 g (1 lb) sugar for each 600 ml (1 pint) extract. Heat gently, stirring, until the sugar has dissolved, then bring to the boil and boil rapidly for about 10–15 minutes or until the setting point is reached. To test for setting point, remove the pan from the heat, drop a tiny amount of the jelly on to a cold saucer, leave to cool, then push the jelly with a finger. If the surface of the jelly wrinkles, the setting point has been reached.
4 Skim the jelly, stir in the mint and add a few drops of green food colouring. Allow to cool slightly, then stir well to distribute the mint.
5 Pour into warmed, sterilised jars, and put waxed discs, wax side down, on the surface of the jelly. Cover immediately with a dampened round of cellophane. Store in a cool place.

Whole Strawberry Jam

There's no better way to serve this jam than with home made scones and clotted cream.

Makes about 2.3 kg (5 lb)
1.1 kg (2½ lb) small strawberries, hulled
45 ml (3 tbsp) lemon juice
1.4 kg (3 lb) sugar
knob of butter
227 ml (8 fl oz) bottle of commercial pectin

1 Place the strawberries in an aluminium or stainless steel preserving pan with the lemon juice and sugar. Leave for 1 hour, stirring occasionally.
2 Heat slowly, stirring, until the sugar has dissolved, then add the knob of butter.
3 Bring to the boil and boil rapidly for 4 minutes, stirring occasionally.
4 Remove the pan from the heat and stir in the pectin. Leave to stand for at least 20 minutes.
5 Pour into warm, sterilised jars, and put waxed discs, wax side down, on the surface of the jelly. Cover immediately with a dampened round of cellophane. Store in a cool place.

Rhubarb Ginger Jam

This is an unusual jam that makes the most of a glut of rhubarb.

Makes about 2 kg (4½ lb)
1.1 kg (2½ lb) rhubarb (prepared weight), chopped
1.1 kg (2½ lb) sugar
juice of 2 lemons
25 g (1 oz) root ginger
100 g (4 oz) stem or crystallised ginger, chopped

1 Place the rhubarb in a large bowl in alternate layers with the sugar and lemon juice, cover and leave overnight.
2 Next day, peel and bruise the root ginger slightly with a weight or rolling pin, and tie it in a piece of muslin. Put the rhubarb mixture in a preserving pan with the muslin bag, bring to the boil and boil rapidly for 15 minutes, stirring frequently.
3 Remove the muslin bag, add the stem or crystallised ginger and boil for a further 5 minutes until setting point is reached. To test for setting point, drop a tiny amount of the jelly on to a cold saucer, leave to cool, then push the jelly with a finger. If the surface of the jelly wrinkles, the setting point of the jelly has been reached. Remove the pan from the heat while carrying out the test.
4 Skim the jam. Pour into warm, sterilised jars, and put waxed discs, wax side down, on the surface of the jelly. Cover immediately with a dampened round of cellophane. Store in a cool place.

Redcurrant Jelly

Redcurrant jelly can be served with any lamb, game or even chicken dish.

1.5 kg (3 lb) redcurrants
sugar

1 Place the currants in a preserving pan with 600 ml (1 pint) water and simmer gently for about 30 minutes until the fruit is very tender.
2 Spoon the pulp into a jelly bag or cloth attached to the legs of an upturned stool, and leave to strain into a clean bowl. Leave to drip naturally without squeezing the bag or cloth as this would make the jelly cloudy.
3 Measure the liquid, pour it back into the pan and add 450 g (1 lb) sugar for each 600 ml (1 pint) liquid. Heat gently, stirring with a wooden spoon, until the sugar has dissolved. Bring to the boil and boil rapidly for 10–15 minutes or until the setting point is reached. To test for setting point, drop a tiny amount of the jelly on to a cold saucer, leave to cool, then push the jelly with a finger. If the surface of the jelly wrinkles, the setting point has been reached. Remove the pan from the heat while carrying out the test.
4 Skim the jelly. Pour into warmed, sterilised jars, and put waxed discs, wax side down, on the surface of the jelly. Cover immediately with a dampened round of cellophane. Store in a cool place.

REDCURRANT JELLY (*page 89*)

TOMATO RELISH (*page 92*)

Marrow and Apple Chutney

Apples and onions are the base of many chutneys.
Here they are combined with marrow.

Makes about 3 kg (6 lb)

2 kg (4 lb) marrow, peeled and chopped
75 g (3 oz) salt
1 kg (2 lb) cooking apples, peeled, cored and finely
chopped
500 g (1 lb) shallots or onions, skinned and chopped
500 g (1 lb) soft brown sugar
1.2 litres (2 pints) distilled vinegar
5 ml (1 tsp) ground ginger
15 g (½ oz) pickling spice

1 Put the marrow pieces into a large bowl in layers with the salt and leave for 12 hours or overnight.
2 Next day, rinse the marrow pieces, drain off the water and put them into a preserving pan. Add the apples, shallots, sugar, vinegar and spice. (If using whole spice, put them into a muslin bag.) Cook gently but steadily, uncovered, for about 2 hours, stirring occasionally, until the mixture is thick. Remove the muslin bag, if used.
3 Pour into pre-heated jars while still warm and cover immediately with airtight and vinegar-proof tops. Store for 2–3 months before eating.

Tomato Relish

A lovely, sharp fresh relish with a light spiciness to
it that is ideal for cold meats.

Makes about 1.4 kg (3 lb)

1.4 kg (3 lb) tomatoes, skinned and sliced
500 g (1 lb) cucumber or marrow, peeled, seeded and
roughly chopped
50 g (2 oz) salt
2 garlic cloves, skinned and finely chopped
1 large red pepper, seeded, cored and roughly chopped
450 ml (¾ pint) malt vinegar
15 ml (1 tbsp) mustard powder
2.5 ml (½ tsp) ground allspice
2.5 ml (½ tsp) mustard seeds

1 Layer the tomatoes and cucumber in a bowl, sprinkle each layer with salt. Cover and leave overnight.
2 Next day, drain and rinse well and place in a large saucepan. Add the garlic and pepper. Blend the vinegar with the dry ingredients, stir into the pan and bring slowly to the boil. Boil gently for about 1 hour, stirring occasionally, until the mixture is soft.
3 Spoon the relish into pre-heated jars and cover immediately with airtight and vinegar-proof tops. Store for 3–4 months before eating.

Pear and Lemon Chutney

❧

A spicy chutney to serve with curries.

❧

Makes about 2 kg (4 lb)

2 kg (4 lb) pears, peeled, cored and chopped
500 g (1 lb) onions, skinned and chopped
375 g (12 oz) seedless raisins, chopped
50 g (2 oz) stem ginger, chopped
grated rind and juice of 2 lemons
250 g (8 oz) soft brown sugar
30 ml (2 tbsp) salt
1.2 litres (2 pints) distilled vinegar
2 garlic cloves, skinned and crushed
6 chillies, crushed
4 whole cloves

❧

1 Place the pears, onions, raisins, ginger, lemon rind and juice, sugar, salt and vinegar in a preserving pan.

2 Tie the garlic, chillies and cloves in a piece of muslin and add to the pan. Bring to the boil, and simmer gently, uncovered, for about 2 hours, stirring occasionally, until the mixture is thick and no excess liquid remains.

3 Remove the muslin bag, spoon the chutney into pre-heated jars and cover immediately with airtight and vinegar-proof tops. Store for 2–3 months before eating.

Piccalilli

❧

Choose crisp, fresh vegetables for this classic pickle.

❧

3 kg (6 lb) mixed marrow, cucumber, beans, small
onions and cauliflower (prepared weight)
375 g (12 oz) salt
275 g (9 oz) granulated sugar
15 ml (1 tbsp) mustard powder
7.5 ml (1½ tsp) ground ginger
2 garlic cloves, skinned and crushed
1.5 litres (2½ pints) distilled vinegar
50 g (2 oz) plain flour
30 ml (2 tbsp) turmeric

❧

1 Seed the marrow and finely dice the marrow and cucumber. Top, tail and slice the beans, skin and halve the onions and break the cauliflower into small florets. Layer the vegetables in a large bowl, sprinkling each layer with salt. Add 3.6 litres (6 pints) water, cover and leave for 24 hours.

2 The next day, remove the vegetables and rinse then drain them well. Blend the sugar, mustard, ginger and garlic with 1 litre (2 pints) of the vinegar in a large pan. Add the vegetables, bring to the boil and simmer for 20 minutes until the vegetables are cooked but still crisp.

3 Blend the flour and turmeric with the remaining vinegar and stir into the cooked vegetables. Bring to the boil and cook for 2 minutes.

4 Spoon into pre-heated jars and cover immediately with airtight and vinegar-proof tops. Store for 2–3 months before eating.

Index